It's another Quality Book from CGP

This book is for anyone studying AQA GCSE Food Technology.

Let's face it, D&T is pretty hard-going — you've got a whole load of technical stuff to learn on top of doing your project.

Happily this CGP book helps to take the headache out of all that learning. We've explained all the technical stuff — and drawn plenty of pictures to make the whole thing that bit clearer. Plus we've stuck in some handy hints to help make your project a winner, and some tips on exam technique.

And in true CGP style it's got some daft bits in to try and make the whole experience at least vaguely entertaining for you.

What CGP is all about

Our sole aim here at CGP is to produce the highest quality books — carefully written, immaculately presented and dangerously close to being funny.

Then we work our socks off to get them out to you — at the cheapest possible prices.

Contents

Section Three — Food Processes

Section Four — Marketing and Environment

Published by CGP

Editors:
Charlotte Burrows, Katherine Craig, Ben Fletcher, Rosie Gillham, Helena Hayes, Sarah Hilton, Ali Palin, Ed Robinson

Contributors:
Marion Brown, Angela Nugent

With thanks to Phillip Holton for the content review.
With thanks to Gemma Hallam and Sharon Keeley for the proofreading.

With thanks to Laura Stoney for the copyright research.

ISBN: 978 1 84762 358 4

Groovy website: www.cgpbooks.co.uk
Jolly bits of clipart from CorelDRAW®

Printed by Elanders Ltd, Newcastle upon Tyne.

Based on the classic CGP style created by Richard Parsons.

Project Advice

Unlike most subjects, in Food Technology you actually get to make something tasty (well, hopefully).

The Project is Worth 60% of your GCSE

1) Your Food Technology project is called 'the controlled assessment'.
2) There are 90 marks available for the project (the folder plus the final product).
3) Your teacher will give you as much help as they're allowed to by the exam board, so do ask them... but mostly it's up to you to make a good job of your project.
4) You can dip into this book for a bit of extra help. Section 1 is all about the design process, so if you're not sure where to start, that might be a good place to look.
5) If you're wondering about a particular detail — what type of sugar to use, say — it's probably quickest to look that up in the index and go straight to that page.

Only Put Relevant Stuff in Your Folder

1) Your teacher will give you plenty of guidance on what needs to go in your folder, but you can use this section of the book for a reminder.
2) The next two pages tell you what you can get marks for and give you a few tips on how to get them.
3) This next bit is really important:

- Don't waffle. Your folder should be about 20 sheets of A3. You'll lose marks if you do much more than that.
- So DON'T waste space on irrelevant stuff, especially at the research stage (see next page).

Include Plenty of Photos

1) DO put in lots of photos. You MUST take photos of your final product, of course. Even the best-looking, most delicious-tasting toad-in-the-hole salad with marmite vinaigrette will be reduced to a foul-smelling puddle if you keep it till the moderator gets round to marking your work.
2) But also, take photos while you're developing your design (see next page)...
3) ...and during the intermediate stages of making your product, to show the making process:

Example

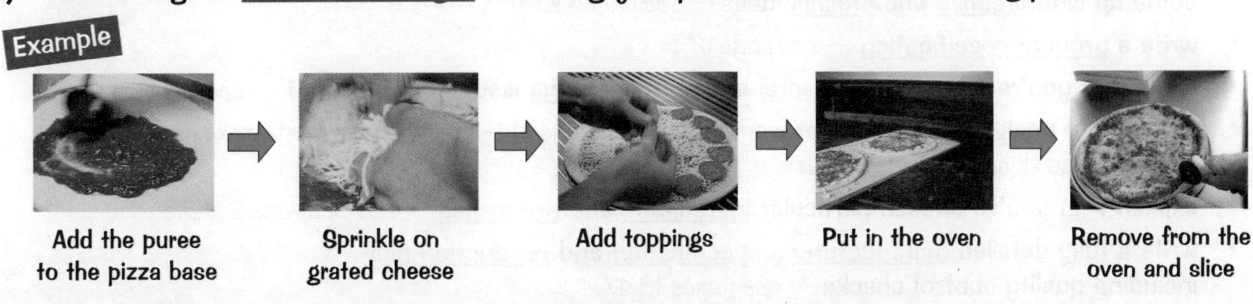

Add the puree to the pizza base → Sprinkle on grated cheese → Add toppings → Put in the oven → Remove from the oven and slice

Controlled Assessment — nope, it's not funny...

When your project is marked, only about a third of the marks are for making the final thing and how good it is. Most of the controlled assessment marks depend on the sheer brilliance of your folder.

Project Advice

The Exam Board Sets the Task

You'll be given a Context and a Design Brief. For example:

Context
Food shopping in 21st-century Britain is a multicultural experience. Shops sell ingredients from around the world, and ready meals are influenced by the traditions of many different countries.

Design Brief
A retirement home decides to have a 'multicultural day', with themed entertainment and food. Design and make a two-course meal that reflects at least two different cultures to serve at the home.

Task Analysis is Worth 8 Marks

You need to show that you've understood the task. To get top marks for the above task you'd have to:

- analyse the context — e.g. show that you understand how cultural differences affect the designing and making of food products (ingredients, methods of cooking, how food is presented...)
- identify and research the target market — e.g. find out what older people are likely to want and need (see pages 6-7 for more on market research)
- analyse existing products — visit shops to research ingredients, look up ideas in recipe books or using the internet... (see pages 4-5 for more on product analysis)
- analyse your research — summarise your findings and say how they'll influence your design (see pages 8-9 for more on research analysis)
- write design criteria (see page 9) — make sure they're based on your research analysis

But remember, this stuff is only worth 8 marks out of 90. The moderators don't want to see more than three A3 sides of research. However they do want you to summarise your findings and they do want you to use your research findings when you write your design criteria.

Development of Proposals is Worth 32 Marks

Your design folder should 'tell the story' of your design. The moderator wants to see how you got from the design criteria to the manufacturer's specification. So, make sure you:

- come up with creative and original ideas — see pages 10-11
- write a product specification — see page 12
- show that you're taking social, moral and environmental issues into account — see Section 4
- model your design and make improvements — see pages 14-15, and remember to take photos of the various things you've tried out
- explain why you've chosen particular ingredients and processes — see Sections 2 and 3
- write a fully detailed manufacturer's specification and production plan, including quality control checks — see pages 16-17

Tell the story of your design — and give it a happy ending...

You'd scarcely believe how much moderators hate wading through pages and pages of recipes that you've copied off the internet. But believe me, you won't get many 'research' marks if that's all you do.

Project Advice

Making is Worth 32 Marks

This is the really fun bit — actually making your product. So enjoy it, but remember:

1) Use all the quality control checks you wrote in your manufacturer's specification. (If you don't, and you make a complete hash of things, you'll only have to start again.)
2) You'll only get top marks if you work accurately and skilfully. So use the right techniques and tools for the job, including CAM if appropriate, and don't be slapdash — it'll show.
3) Remember to take photos during the process, as well as of the finished thing.
4) Don't poison anyone.

Testing and Evaluating is Worth 12 Marks

To get those 12 marks you'll need to:

- test and evaluate your design throughout the designing and making process, taking other people's opinions into account (see pages 14-15)
- refer back to the design criteria and the product specification when you evaluate your ideas and products
- justify (explain why) you're making particular changes to the product
- explain how you'd modify the product for commercial production

Don't just use star diagrams (p7). Moderators see those all the time and they get a bit bored of them.

Communication is Worth 6 Marks

1) Moderators love it when you use the right technical words.
2) They love it even more if you spell things correctly and use good grammar and punctuation.
3) Make sure you've explained things clearly — get someone who knows nothing about your project to read it and see if it makes sense.
4) And remember, you can't get top marks for communication if you write too much or waffle.

Paula was disappointed to hear that her communication system was only worth 6 marks.

But Don't Forget The Exam — It's Worth 40%

1) In the exam you'll be tested on everything you've learned during the course — materials, tools, how to design things, how to make things, health and safety, environmental issues...
2) This book can help you learn all that stuff — and it has questions for you to check what you know.
3) There's a glossary at the back of the book, in case you need to sort out your monosaccharides from your monosodium glutamate.
4) The exam technique section (pages 60 — 63) has some worked examples of exam-style questions, and some hints on how to make sure you get top marks.

Evaluate, evaluate, evaluate...

When you evaluate a design or product, remember to explain which aspects of the design or product need changing and why. It's another little step on the long and winding road to coursework heaven.

Product and Market Analysis

Manufacturers don't often develop a brand new product — they usually redesign an existing one. First, they do a product analysis — on their own or a competitor's product — to find ways to improve it.

Start with Disassembly and Packaging Analysis

Disassembly means taking a product apart and examining the bits. When you do this, take a photo of the packaging and food before you start. And remember to make notes. Write about:

1) The measurements of the product — make a table with the weight of each ingredient in. E.g. If you're disassembling a cheese and tomato sandwich, weigh the cheese, tomato and bread. This will give you the proportions of each thing.

Bread	243 g
Cheese	61 g
Tomato	120 g

There's about four times the weight of bread as cheese.

There's almost twice the weight of tomato as cheese.

2) The textures and colours of the various parts of the product, e.g. "It has a flaky golden crust". *Describe the texture using words like dry, moist, crunchy, creamy, etc.*
3) How the product is put together and how you think it was made, e.g. "The cheese is added last".
4) How it tastes, smells and looks. Be specific, e.g. "It's very bitter" (not "It's horrible").

The packaging is also useful — it shows you more detail about the product.

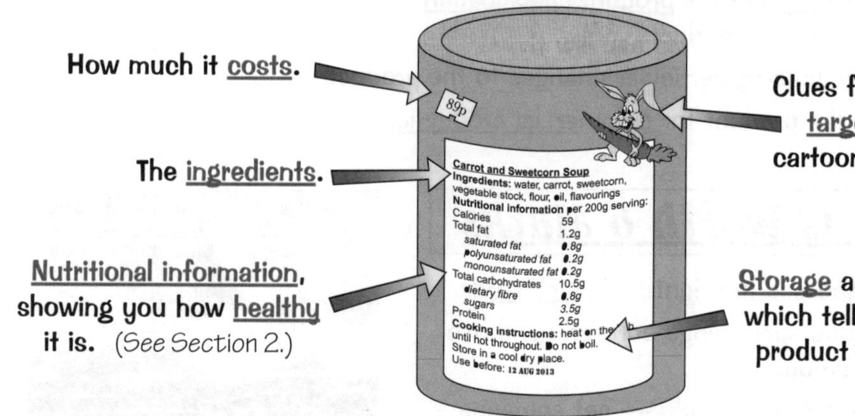

How much it costs.

The ingredients.

Nutritional information, showing you how healthy it is. *(See Section 2.)*

Clues from the style about the target market, e.g. using cartoons to target young kids.

Storage and cooking instructions, which tell you where to keep the product and how to prepare it.

Use the Info to Make Your Product Better

After you've analysed a product, decide its faults and find ways to make yours better. Think about:

1) The quality, quantity and proportions of the ingredients.
2) The size, shape, weight, appearance, texture and flavour.
3) The quality and effectiveness of the packaging.
4) The price — if you think it's too expensive for what it is, say why, and by how much.
5) The nutritional value.

"Brilliant! Sausage with eggs, I bet no one's ever thought of that before..."

When you write out how to make it better, be clear and exact.

E.g. If you reckon the original looks a bit pale and unappealing, don't just say "make it look nicer" — say something like "make sure the cheese topping is golden brown in colour".

Get me a drill — prepare to be disassembled, Mr Scone...

Ah, there's nothing like being critical. And there's loads to think about and try to improve — maybe the food could be cooked or stored differently, perhaps it should be aimed at a different target market...

Product and Market Analysis

Before you design anything, you need to find out what people want. This information is dead important in helping you decide what your product should be like. Give the public what they want — simple as that.

Decide Who Your Target Group is

Even the very best products aren't everyone's cup of tea — some people like them and some don't.
Your target group is the group of people you want to sell your product to.
You should ask that group of people what they want the product to be like.

You can group people by things like age, gender, job, hobbies, lifestyle, income, or anything else — it'll probably be a combination of a few of these things.

For example... if you're trying to sell an organic reduced-fat meat substitute, you may decide to target it at middle-aged vegetarians who are trying to lose weight.

But if it's a caviar-filled isotonic garlic burger, you'd probably aim for rich adrenaline-junkies from France.

Think Carefully About What You Want to Find Out

Once you've decided on your target group, you need to decide what to ask them. You could find out:

1) Some information about the person answering your questions. This could help you make sure they're within your target group, or give you extra info.
   - Are they male or female? (probably best to judge for yourself rather than asking...)
   - What age bracket are they in? (11-15, 16-20, 21-25 etc)
   - What job or hobbies do they have?
2) Do they already buy the kind of product you're thinking of developing?
3) Do they like a particular flavour or colour?
4) When and where do they buy it and where do they consume it? This could affect the packaging you use.
5) Will they want to buy your version of the product? Explain the advantage of your product over existing brands — would that be enough to tempt them to buy your version?
6) Is there something they would like from your product that existing brands don't have?

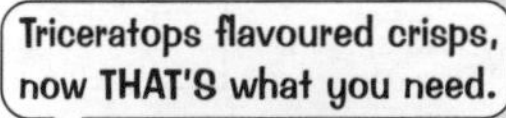

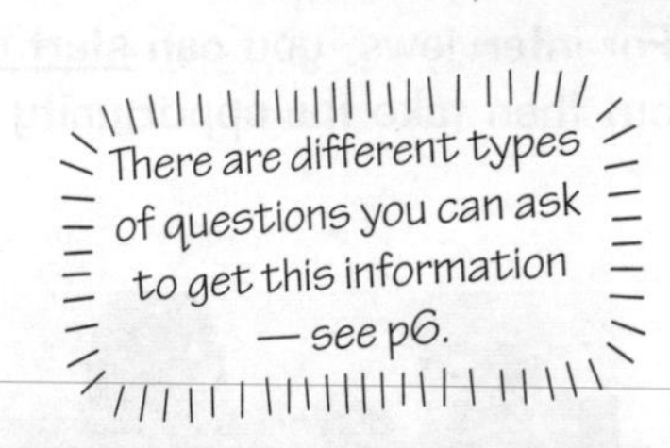

Practice Questions

1) What does "disassembly" mean?
2) List three useful things you can find on the packaging of a food product.
3) Name five faults you might find in an existing product that you could improve on.
4) a) What is a target group?
   b) What features can you use to describe a target group?
   c) List five sensible things you could ask a target group if you were making a new kind of salad.
5) Imagine you are designing a new kind of soup. Write down three pieces of information you'd want to find out from your target group before you start.

Market Research

So you've got your target group and decided what info you need from them.
But how to phrase those all-important questions...

Questionnaires are Forms for People to Fill In

When you write a questionnaire, you should include:

1) A title — for example it could be 'Questionnaire Researching Favourite Puddings'.
2) A brief explanation of the purpose of the questionnaire.
3) A mixture of question types and not too many questions, so people don't get bored and give up answering them.

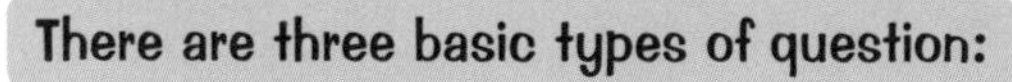

1) Closed Questions — these have a limited number of possible answers, e.g. do you like puddings? Analysing the results is easy for this type of question, e.g. by using graphs or charts.
2) Open Questions — these have no set answer, e.g. why is that your favourite pudding? They give people a chance to provide details and opinions.
   This type of questioning is more time-consuming and it's harder to draw conclusions from the results. But you could gain valuable information.
3) Multiple choice questions — these give a choice of answers. Sometimes the person answering can pick more than one.

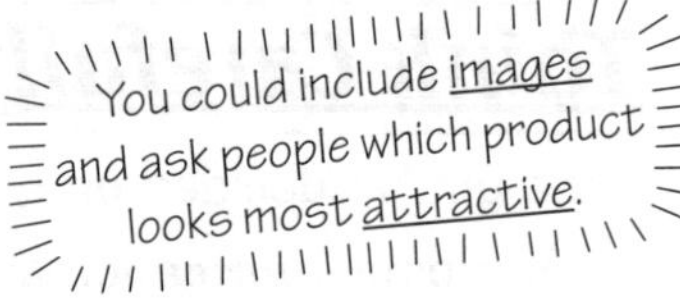

Q4. What kind of puddings do you like?

Chocolate puddings ☑ Ice cream ☐ Slug puddings ☑

Interviews are Face-to-Face Conversations

1) For interviews, you can start off by asking the same sort of questions as in questionnaires — but then take the opportunity to ask follow-up questions, based on the answers you get.

"I can't STAND the smell of tuna..."

2) Get your interviewees to give you extra information to explain their answers — this might help you get more ideas for your product. E.g. if their favourite pudding is trifle, ask them why they like it.
3) Interviews can give you more detailed information than questionnaires — you can have short conversations with people you're aiming to sell to. Just make sure you stick to the point.
4) A problem with interviews is that it's sometimes more difficult to analyse the results than with questionnaires (see p8 for more on analysis) because you might have asked different people different 'follow-up' questions.

I've got it — chocolate packaging and a cardboard cake...

Can you believe all this effort goes into a humble custard tart? Mind you, if they put all this effort into improving food, then why does somebody still make pickled haddock with curry and pineapple sauce?

Market Research

Use Sensory Analysis to Find Out What People Like

Sensory analysis is tasting samples of food and rating how good they are. Manufacturers ask consumers to do it, to find out what they think about new or existing products. This helps the manufacturer decide what characteristics their new product should have. There are different types of test:

1) Ranking or Rating Testing

People are asked to rank a number of similar products, or give them a rating:

Ranking Test	Name: Delia Quiff
Taste the samples and place them in order of preference	
Sample code	Order of Preference
SPE12	2
SPE14	1

Rating system using symbols

Circle the appropriate symbol

Hedonic Scale
1 = Hate
2 = Dislike
3 = It's OK
4 = Like
5 = Love

2) Star Diagrams

Testers rate the main characteristics of a product on a scale of 1-5. Each leg of the diagram represents a characteristic. The marks are then joined up, showing which aspects people like and which they don't.

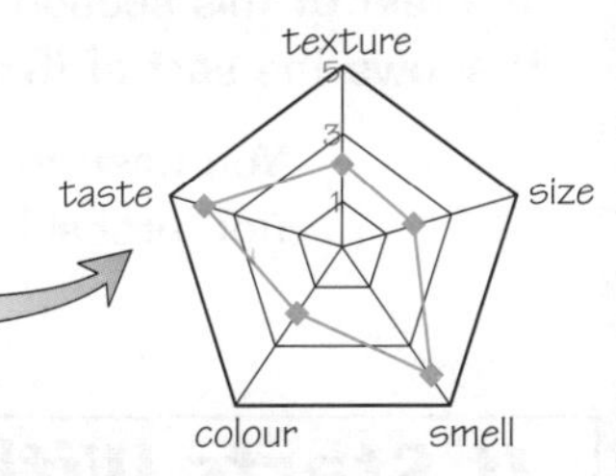

3) Triangle Testing

- This is when testers are given three samples and asked to say which is the "odd one out".
- Manufacturers use it if they're trying to develop a cheap or low-fat version of a food that tastes the same as the original. People taste two samples of the original and one of the new version — but they aren't told which is which.
- If most of the testers correctly pick out the new version, you'll need to re-design the product. But if they can't work out which one is different, you know you've designed a good alternative.

Do Your Sensory Analysis Properly

You need a group of people to be testers — ideally people from the target group.

1) Use a quiet area and give tasters water to sip to separate the tastes of different products.
2) Use small amounts of food and clean spoons. Don't let people put used spoons in the food.
3) Use codes or symbols for the products, to make sure the tasters aren't influenced by the name.
4) Make sure the tasters understand what they're meant to do.

Practice Questions

1) Imagine you are researching opinions about a new sandwich product. Write one example of:
a) a closed question b) an open question c) a multiple choice question
2) Give one advantage and one disadvantage of interviews compared to questionnaires.
3) What's the point of sensory analysis?
4) Briefly describe three different types of sensory analysis.
5) The Star Diagram on the right shows the results of some sensory analysis on a new sandwich product you've designed. Based on these results:
a) What aspects about the sandwich would you try to change?
b) What aspects would you keep the same?

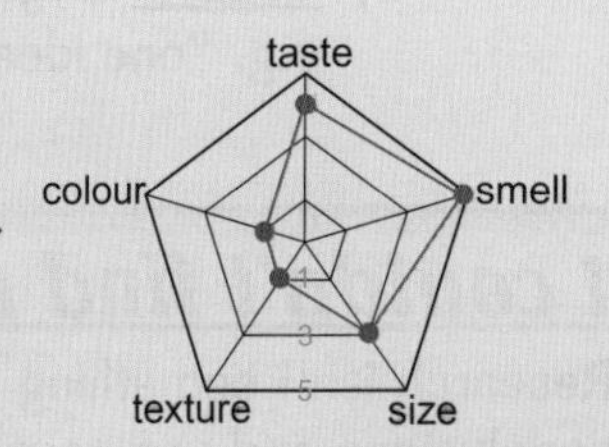

Design Criteria

The process of designing and making something is called 'the design process' (gosh). The whole process can take a while — so, like many pineapples, it's usually broken down into smaller chunks.

The Design Process is Similar in Industry and School

The things you'll have to do for your project and for the design question in the exam are pretty similar to what happens in industry. Remember:

- The best products are those that address a real need.
- That's why companies spend so much time and money on consumer research. The more people there are who would actually use a product, the more chance the product has of being a roaring success.

The rest of this section describes a typical design process.
It shows the sort of thing that happens in industry every day.

You need to understand the overall process, even though you probably won't have to actually do every bit of it.

It Starts With a Design Brief

The design brief explains why there's a need for a new product. It usually includes:

1) an outline of the context (background) and who it involves (the target group)
2) what kind of product is needed
3) how the product will be used

The Design Brief is short and to-the-point — it's basically a starting point for the development of the product.

Do Research to Draw Conclusions

The design brief will help you decide which products to analyse and what you need to find out from your market research. When you've done this research (see pages 6-7) you should have loads of info. Then you have to use the information to help with your design.

1) Summarise what you've found out — pick out the most important and useful findings, e.g. "hedgehogs are a popular ingredient in breakfast cereals".
2) Explain what impact the research will have on your designs, e.g. "hedgehogs will be a major ingredient".
3) Suggest ways forward from the research you've done, e.g. "one idea would be to add spines to the cereal".

I couldn't find my pen the first time, so I'm researching...

Research isn't something you do just for the sake of it — it's really important that you draw useful conclusions and use your findings to help you decide what your product is going to be like.

Design Criteria

Ideas, ideas, ideas... but where's the beef? (Or, indeed, the lard?) Time to start thinking about what qualities your product is going to bring to the table.

You Need a List of Design Criteria

1) **The conclusions from your market research should show what kind of characteristics your product needs to have.**
2) **These requirements are your design criteria.** (A list of design criteria is sometimes called a design specification.)
3) **Each point says one thing about what the product should be like, e.g.**

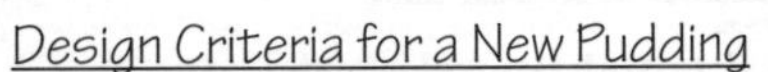

Design Criteria for a New Pudding
- attractive topping
- chocolate-flavoured
- big enough to feed 8 people

4) **You don't have to be really exact at this point — that comes later (see page 12). Just a few words for each point is enough.**
5) **But you do need to show how the criteria are related to your research — e.g. it's fair enough to have "the omelette should be hexagonal" as one of your criteria, but only if your research analysis concludes that people want a hexagonal omelette — don't just make it up because it sounds interesting.**

EXAM TIP
In the exam, you're given both the Design Brief and Design Criteria. Read them really carefully and highlight the key points.

Practice Questions

1) **Why do companies think consumer research is so important?**
2) **What information does a design brief give? Why is it important?**
3) **Read these questionnaire results about pasta and write two brief conclusions based on them:**

Q1. What is your favourite type of pasta?
Answers:

tagliatelle 10%
penne 16%
spaghetti 42%
ravioli 32%

Q2. Which is more important when eating pasta — taste or healthiness?
Answers:

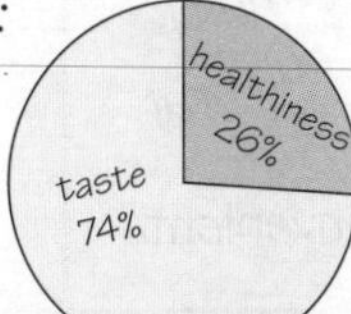

4) **What are design criteria?**
5) **Read this research summary about desserts and make a short list of possible design criteria based on it:**

Most people prefer chocolate flavoured desserts to fruit flavoured ones. However, they are worried that these might not be healthy — the majority want the product to be low in calories, but still to taste very sweet and chocolatey. Texture is also important — runny desserts are less popular than more solid ones.

Generating Proposals

Now hold on to your hats, my wild young things — this is the creative bit.
Time to start generating lots of ideas.

There are a few Tricks that can help you Get Started

1) Work from an existing product or recipe — but change some of its features or production methods so that it fits in with your design criteria.
2) Or you could do a spot of brainstorming...

EXAM TIP
You could get a question asking for initial ideas — just do them as freehand sketches, and if it's worth 5 marks, include 5 details.

Brainstorm to Produce Initial Ideas

1) First, think up key words, questions and initial thoughts about your product. Write down the design criteria and research conclusions too.
2) Don't be too critical at this stage — let your imagination run wild. Even if an idea sounds ridiculous, put it down anyway.
3) Be creative and get as many ideas as you can. Afterwards, decide which ones are good (and so are worth developing) and which ones are as stupid as a wooden blancmange.
4) Use word association — choose a product and write down any related words. E.g. biscuits, mouse, straws, melt and smelly are all associated with...cheese.

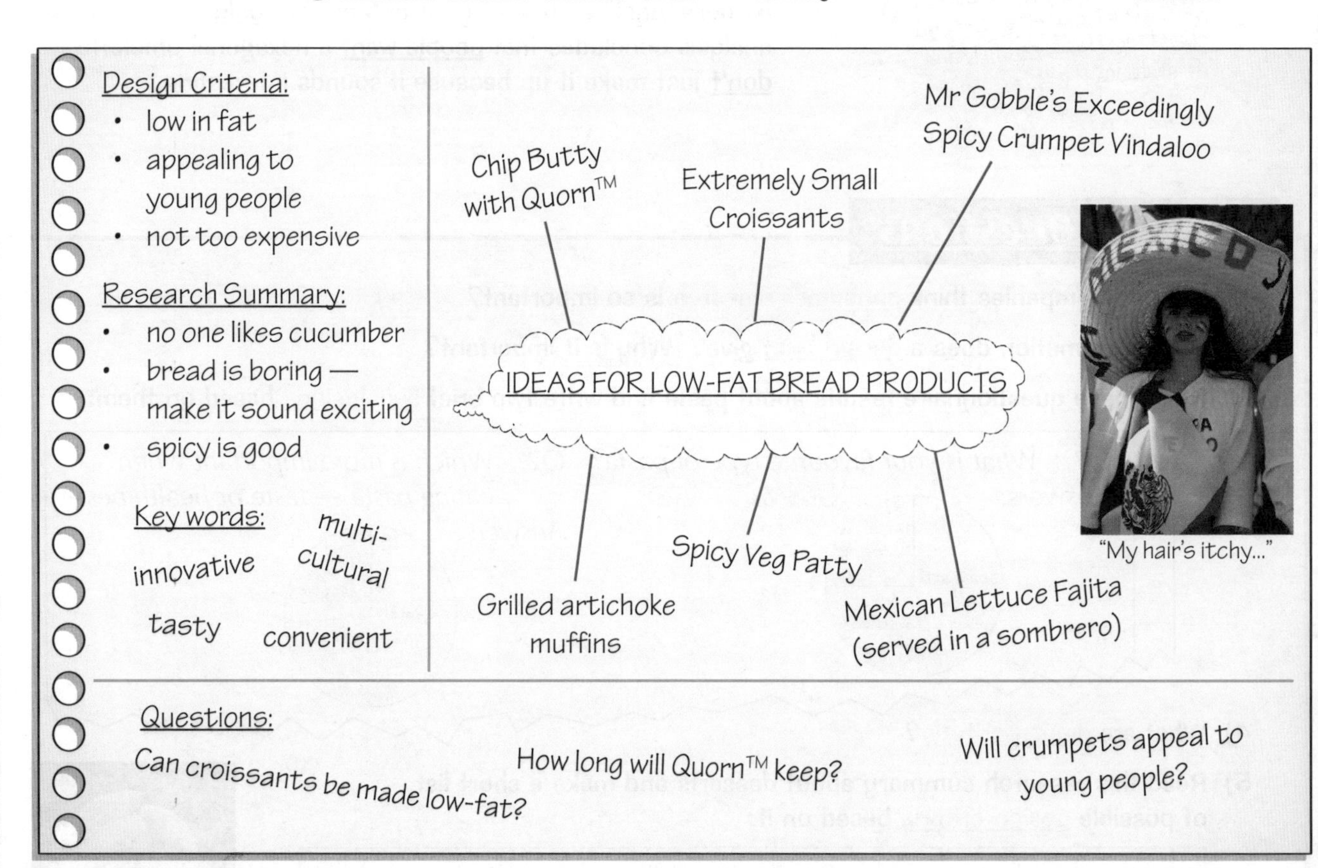

"My hair's itchy..."

It's not wise to torch food — don't blow your own crumpet...

Try to think of a range of ideas that are really different from each other. Then you might be able to combine the best features from a few of them and get the most delicious meal since Ostrich Madras.

Generating Proposals

You need to Come up with a Range of Designs

1) Once you've sorted out the good ideas from the bad ones, annotate (i.e. add notes to) each good design idea to fully explain what it is and why it's good. You could mention:
   - materials
   - user
   - cost
   - sizes
   - shape
   - advantages / disadvantages

Your notes should link these features to your design criteria.

2) You need to produce a range of different solutions — about 3 or 4 — that meet the design criteria.
3) It's also important that you think you could actually make them — don't go overboard on exciting ideas that you could never produce for real.

Present Your Ideas Clearly

1) To present your ideas, it's usually best to keep it simple — a freehand sketch will do fine, as long as it's clear.

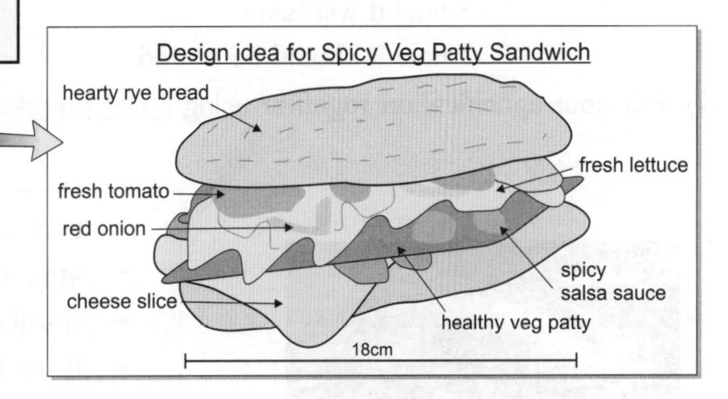

2) Once you've got a few possible designs, have a good think about them all, and decide which is the best idea — i.e. the one that most closely matches the design brief and design criteria. This is the one you should develop.
3) You should check that the nutritional content of your chosen product meets your design criteria too, e.g. if it should be low in fat, check that it is. You could do this using nutritional analysis software:

- The software creates a computer model of your product, from your recipe.
- It calculates the nutritional content of your ingredients and any nutritional losses due to cooking.
- It also tells you the recommended guidelines for your target market, so it's easy to see if you need to adjust your recipe to fit your design brief. Remember, any changes you make will affect the product in other ways too, e.g. the taste.

It's a good idea to carry out nutritional analysis throughout the development process too (see p14). If you modify the recipe, the nutritional content will change too — so you need to keep a check on it as you go along.

See page 43 for more on using computers to help with designing.

Practice Questions

1) Describe two ways of coming up with ideas for a new product.
2) What should you do after you've come up with plenty of ideas?
3) Sketch three possible ideas for products based on the following design brief:

> **Context:** Hot snack for teenagers to eat at school lunch time
> **Product to be developed:** Sandwich or wrap with filling
> **Design criteria:** The product must:
> - be healthy and filling
> - be affordable
> - not require cutlery or a plate

4) How do you know which of your ideas is the best one to develop?
5) What could you use to check the nutritional content of your product?

Product Specification

Once you've picked out the best idea to develop, you're ready to put together a product specification. So put that lard away... you're not ready to do anything practical yet.

The Product Specification Describes the Product

1) The product specification expands on your chosen idea and says exactly what the product is, not just what it tries to do.
2) It describes what the product contains, how it looks and tastes and so on. It should have exact figures and measurements.
3) In your product specification, include some or all of the following:
    - how it will look
    - how it will taste
    - how it should be stored
    - size and weight
    - safety points
    - costs
4) Put your specification together using bullet points, rather than wordy explanations.

- Each sandwich will weigh 180-200 grams.
- Manufacturing cost will be under 75p per unit.
- It will use brown bread.
- It will have a ham, cheese and cucumber filling.
- The primary flavour will be cheese, with a spicy after-taste.

Use words like "will", "should" and "must" in your specification.

EXAM TIP
Your product specification does NOT say how to make it — that goes in the Manufacturer's Specification (see pages 16-17).

Make Sure it's Realistic

1) For your project, you'll have to actually make the product according to the product specification — so all your requirements need to be things you're capable of producing.
2) Once you've got a product specification, you'll need to compare it to the design criteria and confirm that each point is satisfied.

Some points will be harder to check than others. For example, if one of your design criteria is "must be very sweet", you'll have to actually make the product before you can check (by tasting) whether it's sweet enough. It's a good idea to take photos of any taste testing you do.

So many specifications, my head hurts, why why why...

If I told you that product specifications were going to get your pulse racing, I'd be lying. To be honest, they're a bit dull. But it's a vital step in designing and manufacturing a new product. So do it.

Product Specification

Protect Your Design Ideas so YOU Benefit From Them

Let's say you've come up with the ultimate design idea for your food product — something that's not been thought of before but you reckon will be dead popular. Celery and chocolate cheesecake, that sort of thing. There's nothing to stop someone else from taking your idea, developing the product and making loads of money themselves — or is there...

1) If you design a food product that's original (never been done before) then you can legally own your idea, just like you own physical property — it's called intellectual property (IP).

2) You can register different features of your design idea as intellectual property. This means these features are protected — they can't be stolen by anyone else.

3) If your idea is protected, it gives you exclusive rights to develop your product and hopefully go on to make tons of money from it. If someone else wants to do the same thing, they need your permission and they have to pay you for it.

4) If you don't protect a design idea that turns out to be successful, anyone else can copy your idea and benefit from it.

5) You can register the shape, colour, texture and all kinds of other stuff about your design idea. This can include a new ingredient you're using, the recipe, the production process or the product packaging. E.g. In 1937, Coca-Cola registered the design for their cola bottle — so no-one else could copy it.

6) You can only protect your ideas for about 20-25 years — after this, anyone can develop them.

Crikey, I've got it — cheese, it's the missing ingredient for my cake...

EXAM TIP
Try to write one point for each mark in the exam question — e.g. six points for six marks.

Practice Questions

1) Choose the best one of the ideas you sketched for Question 3 on page 11. Write a product specification based on this idea.

2) Why is it a good idea to protect your design ideas?

3) Can other manufacturers use your design idea if you have protected it?

4) Give three examples of features of a product that you could register as intellectual property.

Development

So you've decided which idea to develop and written a product specification, but that doesn't mean it's all done and dusted. Now you need to try it out — make the product — and then make improvements to it.

You can Develop your Design in Different Ways

Depending on the type of product that's being produced, there are a few ways you can develop it.

1) You could make some more detailed sketches. This might help you decide on some of the smaller details you hadn't thought about before, e.g. how the different toppings of a pizza would be arranged.
2) Do some practical experimentation with different aspects of the design, e.g. you could try using soft brown sugar instead of caster sugar, or try grilling rather than baking. Trying out different versions of your design is called modelling — and each different version is a model. (See below for more on modelling.)
3) Use other people's opinions about developments to help you give them what they want.

"This time I'll try using a spoon to mix it instead of using my fingers."

Make Changes and Compare Models

1) After you've made the first real version of your design idea, you need to do some tests to check it's how you wanted it to be — this is called evaluation.
2) These tests could cover appearance, texture, taste, smell or other things. Check it against all the design criteria too.

If your product is for freezing and reheating, you'll need to try doing that — and then evaluate the product after reheating.

It's dead important that your sensory analysis and other tests are thorough and rigorous — you need to be super-critical of your models so that you can make the final product as good as possible.

3) You'll probably find there are some things in your initial design that didn't work out the way you'd hoped — maybe it tasted great but was really expensive, in which case you could try using some cheaper ingredients or making a smaller product.
4) The evaluation of the first model might give you ideas about what modifications are worth a try. So make the changes and try again. Use a digital camera to record each model you make.
5) Put each model you make through the same tests. That way you can compare them fairly and see if you've actually improved things.

The sponge cake wasn't greasy enough, so in the next model I'm going to try using lard instead of butter.

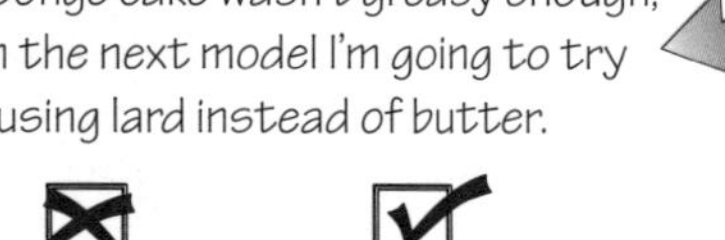

Development is a vital part of the design process. Ideally you should solve all the potential problems with your design at this stage.

Dehydrated water — it's got to be a winner...

Modelling and evaluation go hand in hand. It's pointless baking a cake and eating it if you're not going to bother learning anything from it. Ah, well... maybe not actually. If it's a really big cake.

Development

Keep Going Until You Get it Just Right

You might have to modify quite a few aspects of your design. For example, you could try changing:

1) The ingredients you use (or what proportions you use, or how you combine them) — see page 39.
2) The shape or size of the product — you could use try using a different shaped tin for a cake, say.
3) The finish — for example you could add a glaze, or grill something briefly to brown it on top.

Changing one thing might mean you need to change something else.

For example, say you bake a cake in a wide, circular tin instead of a deep, loaf-shaped tin. The cake will now be thinner and could burn more easily... so you might have to alter the cooking time or temperature.

Here's a summary of how it works every time you try something new:

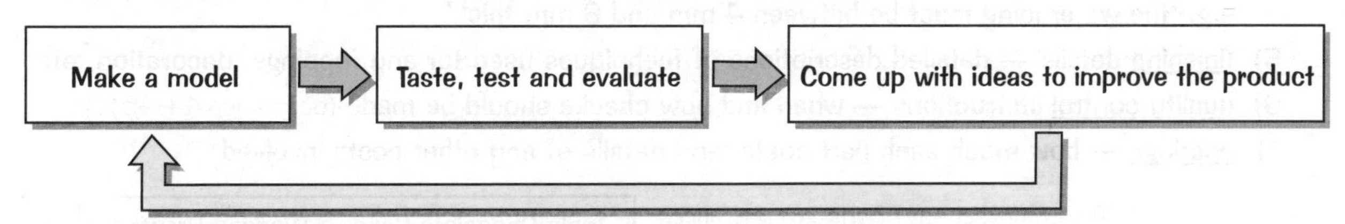

1) You might have to change your product specification to make sure you meet the design criteria. That's fine — the whole point of development is to find out what works and what doesn't.
2) But you can't change the design specification/criteria — because then you probably wouldn't be meeting the design brief any more.
3) In other words, you've got to make your product fit the design criteria, not the other way round.

Practice Questions

1) This young man is doing a spot of modelling. What does modelling mean in Food Technology?

2) Imagine you are developing a new type of sponge pudding that has to be tasty but low in fat. You make the first version of the product.
   a) Describe three tests you could use as part of your evaluation (see p7).
   b) Assume the product fails each test, so you try changing the ingredients. Suggest two other changes you could try.
3) What should you aim to have done by the time you finish your development?
   A made every possible spaghetti dish
   B solved all the potential problems with your product
   C obtained a sample of Antony Worrall-Thompson's beard
4) Imagine you are making a new kind of low-cost pizza, but your first model's texture is too dry. Describe three ways you could try developing your product to improve the texture.
5) a) What type of specification might change as you make different models of your product?
   b) What type of specification stays the same?

Manufacturer's Specification

When you know exactly what you're going to make and how, you need to communicate all that info to the person who's actually going to make it — the manufacturer. (In the controlled assessment you're the manufacturer, but don't relax — you still need to do all this stuff, and it could be in the exam.)

You Need to Make a Manufacturer's Specification

A manufacturer's specification can be a series of written statements, or working drawings and sequence diagrams. It should include enough detail for someone else to make the product — stuff like:

1) how to make it — a clear description of each stage, which may include photos
2) a list of ingredients with precise amounts of each
3) the dimensions of the product, given in millimetres
4) tolerances — the maximum and minimum sizes or weights for each part, e.g. 'the water icing must be between 4 mm and 6 mm thick'
5) finishing details — detailed descriptions of techniques used for any toppings, decoration, etc
6) quality control instructions — when and how checks should be made (see pages 44-45)
7) costings — how much each part costs, and details of any other costs involved

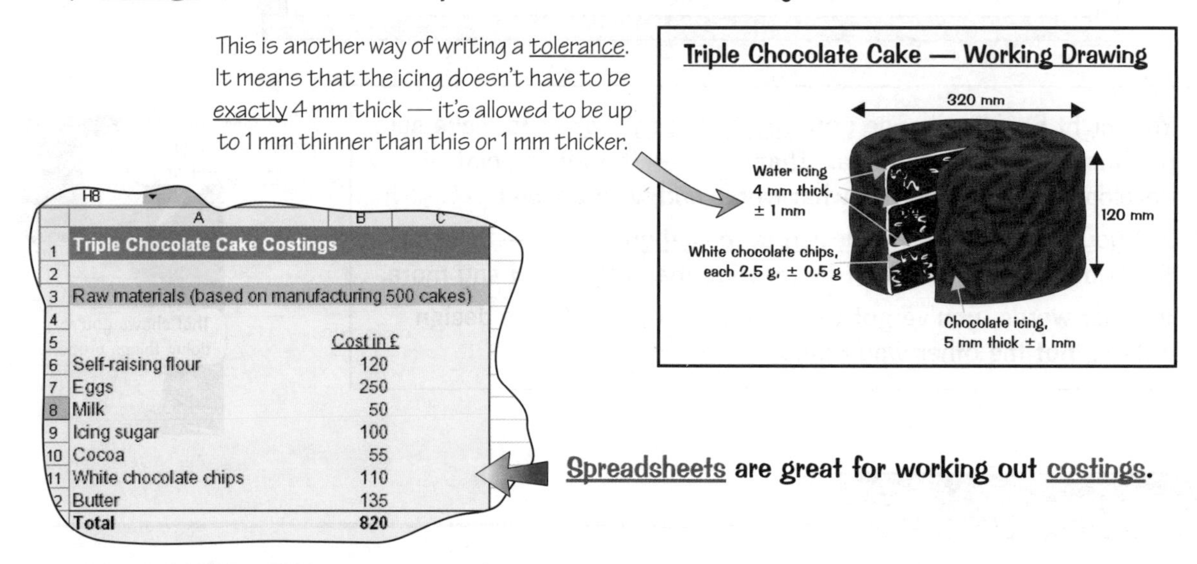

	A	B
1	Triple Chocolate Cake Costings	
2		
3	Raw materials (based on manufacturing 500 cakes)	
4		
5		Cost in £
6	Self-raising flour	120
7	Eggs	250
8	Milk	50
9	Icing sugar	100
10	Cocoa	55
11	White chocolate chips	110
12	Butter	135
	Total	820

Plan How Long the Production Process Should Take

When you get to this stage of product development, you also need to plan:

1) any changes needed to make it suitable for mass-production
2) how long each stage will take
3) what needs to be prepared before you can start each stage
4) how you'll ensure consistency and quality

See the next page as well for some different ways to help with this planning.

Manufacturer's specification — lard, lard and more lard...

You know what they say... the devil's in the detail. Yeah, well, I don't know exactly what that means, but it's probably got something to do with being really precise. And that's what you've got to do with your manufacturer's specification, or your masterpiece could end up as a dog's dinner.

Manufacturer's Specification

Manufacturing a product takes a shedload of careful planning.

Use Charts to Help You

You need to work out what order to do things in. It's also important to work out how long each stage will take and how these times will fit into the total time you've allowed for production.

1) Work Order This can be produced as a table or flow chart. The purpose is to plan each task in sequence. You should include quality control checks.

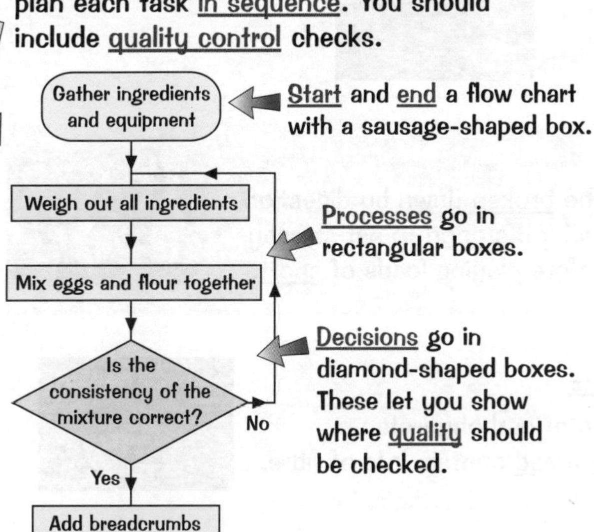

Start and end a flow chart with a sausage-shaped box.

Processes go in rectangular boxes.

Decisions go in diamond-shaped boxes. These let you show where quality should be checked.

2) Gantt Chart This is a time plan. The tasks are listed in order down the left-hand side, and the timing plotted across the top. The coloured squares show how long each task takes.

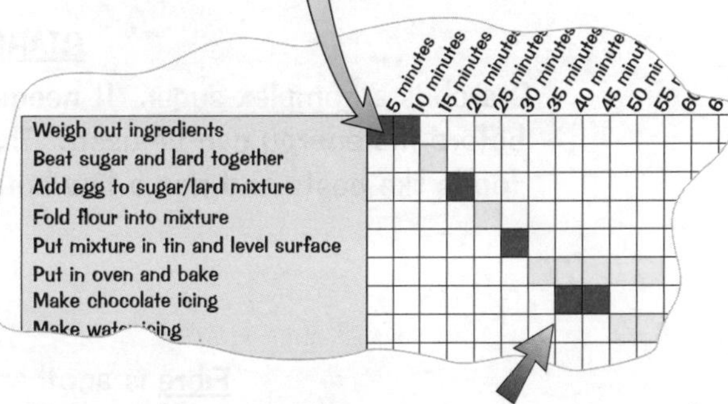

Some tasks can overlap, e.g. you can get on with making the icing while the cake is in the oven.

Test The Finished Product

When you think you've got the final product, it's vital to photograph and test it. You have to make sure it meets the original design criteria (see page 9).

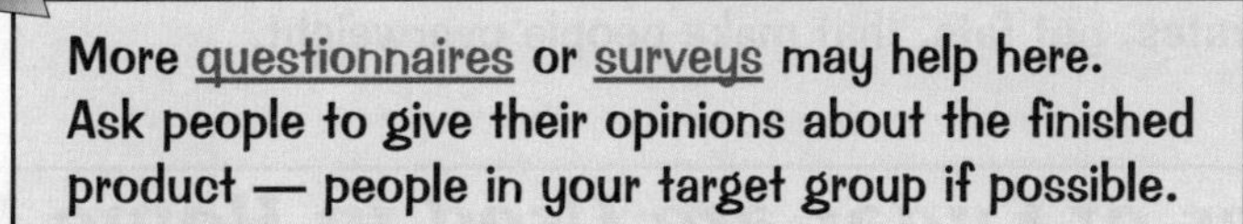
More questionnaires or surveys may help here. Ask people to give their opinions about the finished product — people in your target group if possible.

Practice Questions

1) Make a working drawing and ingredients list for a cheese and lettuce sandwich.

2) The manufacturer's specification for a batch of fairy cakes says that each cake must weigh 52 g ± 3 g. Explain what this means.

3) How do each of these help your planning?
   a) a flow chart
   b) a Gantt Chart

4) Make the following:
   a) a flow chart for boiling an egg
   b) a Gantt chart for making Spaghetti Bolognese

5) What things should you check when you reckon you've got the final product?

Carbohydrates — Sugar

Carbohydrates are one of the major food groups. Get your teeth into this...

Carbohydrates are Needed for Energy

Carbohydrates are split into three types: sugar, starch and fibre.

SUGAR

Includes simple sugars like glucose and fructose, as well as double sugars such as lactose and sucrose. They're easier to digest than starch.

STARCH

Starch is a complex sugar. It needs to be broken down by digestion before the energy can be used. That's why it's good to eat starchy foods like pasta and rice a few hours before playing loads of sport.

FIBRE

Fibre is another type of carbohydrate. Bran, fruit, beans and brown bread contain lots of fibre.

Here's some sciency mumbo-jumbo — it's all to do with the chemical structure:

simple sugars = monosaccharides (the most basic sugar molecules)
double sugars = disaccharides (made up of 2 monosaccharides)
complex sugars = polysaccharides } long chains of monosaccharides)
fibres = non-starch polysaccharides (NSPs) } (long chains of monosaccharides)

Carbohydrates are good sources of energy. But energy that's not used is stored by the body as fat. So it's often carbohydrates, not fats, that make people overweight.

Several Types of Sugar are Used in Home Baking

1) Granulated sugar is for general kitchen use, e.g. to sweeten tea or breakfast cereal.
2) Caster sugar has finer crystals than granulated sugar. It's used for baking, especially cakes and biscuits, which need to have a fine texture.
3) Brown sugars — demerara and muscovado are brown sugars with strong, distinctive flavours. These are used in rich fruit cakes, gingerbread and Christmas puddings.
4) Icing sugar is a white, powdery sugar used for icing and sweets.

Most of these originally come from sugar cane.
Sugar also naturally occurs in things like fruit and honey.

My parrot loves starch — she's called Polly Saccharide...

Sugar is obviously good in some ways — it tastes great, and you get sweets, cakes, biscuits, chocolates and all things good from it. But it rots your teeth. Though I don't miss mine *that* much.

Carbohydrates — Sugar

You might think that sugar is just used in desserts and sickly sweet things. Well, you'd be wrong — WRONG, I tell you, *WRONG!* (cue maniacal laughter). It's used in all sorts of foods.

Sugar is Used in Loads of Food Products

Sugar is used widely in food manufacturing, even in savoury products.
Just look on some ingredients labels — fructose, dextrose, sucrose, inverted sugar, maltose, lactose and glucose are all sugars.
Sugar has lots of functions:

My god! This stuff's everywhere... Help me somebody... help!

1) It makes things sweet (obviously) or 'softens' very sharp flavours, e.g. in lemony desserts.
2) It acts as a preservative, e.g. in jam.
3) In creamed mixtures, sugar is beaten with fat, which aerates the mixture (adds air to it) and helps lighten it, e.g. in cakes.
4) It speeds up fermentation, e.g. in bread.
5) Sugar adds colour, e.g. in cakes, biscuits and pastries.
6) Sugar can be heated until it becomes a sweet-tasting, brownish liquid — this is called caramelisation. It's used to top off desserts.

Sugar Substitutes are Sometimes Healthier

1) Sugar substitutes can be used to sweeten drinks and foods.
2) They're better for your teeth than sugar and contain far fewer calories, so they're good for people who are on a slimming diet. They're also good for diabetics, who have to control their sugar intake.
3) Sugar substitutes shouldn't be used for home baking because they don't have the same properties as cane sugar, described above.

Practice Questions

1) What's another name for glucose and fructose?
2) Why is starch a good thing to eat a few hours before running a marathon?
3) What happens if you eat loads of carbohydrates but don't use the energy?
4) Name four types of sugar that you can use if you're making a nice meal for your friends at home.
5) Explain why sugar is used in the following foods:
   a) jam
   b) bread
   c) biscuits
6) Give two reasons why people might use sugar substitutes.

Carbohydrates — Starch

Because of starch's properties, it has a variety of uses. (And not just in food — it's the traditional way to stiffen shirt collars, for instance. But I don't suppose the Food Tech examiner will be terribly interested in that.)

Starch can alter the Structure of Foods

STARCH IS USED AS A BULKING AGENT
Starch granules swell when a liquid is added, and so can provide the bulk of a product, e.g. the starch in flour makes up most of the volume of pasta.

STARCH IS USED AS A GELLING AGENT
When moisture is added to starch granules and heat is applied:

1) Starch granules begin to absorb the liquid and swell.
2) At 80 °C the starch particles break open, making the mixture thick and viscous. This is gelatinisation.
3) Gelatinisation is completed when the liquid reaches 100 °C.
4) The thickened liquid now forms a gel.
5) On cooling, the gel solidifies and takes the form of the container it's in.

Starch is used to Thicken Foods

STARCH IS USED AS A THICKENING AGENT
Sauces and gravies are often made using starch (in flour) and liquid. The thickness depends on the proportions of starch and liquid.

1) The starch and liquid are mixed together.
2) The starch particles form a suspension — they don't dissolve.
3) The mixture is stirred to keep the particles suspended.
4) Heat is applied and gelatinisation occurs, which causes thickening.

STARCH IS USED IN MANUFACTURED PRODUCTS
Modified starch (see next page) is used to thicken things like instant desserts, whipped cream, yoghurts and packet soup. Usually a liquid is added to the starch and it is stirred or whisked.

I love starch too — more than I love eating my toenails...

Interesting starch fact (#1 in a series of 1): modified starch from barley has similar properties to fat and could be used to make stuff like low fat cakes or biscuits. Hmm — but where's the fun in that...

Carbohydrates — Starch

What's that you say? You want to know more about starch? Well, it is pretty thrilling stuff...

Modified Starches are Called Smart Starches

You can get some starches that have been treated so that they react in a particular way in certain conditions. They're known as modified starches or smart starches.

1) Pre-gelatinised starch thickens instantly when mixed with hot water, e.g. packet custard, instant noodles.
2) When protein is heated it can coagulate (become more solid) and squeeze out the fat and water. This is called syneresis. Some starches allow products to be reheated with no syneresis. This is handy with frozen foods (e.g. lasagne) so that they keep their moisture and nutrients when they're cooked.
3) Normal starches can be affected by acid, so that they don't work properly. But some modified starches are immune to it, so they can be used to thicken acidic products, e.g. salad cream, which contains vinegar.

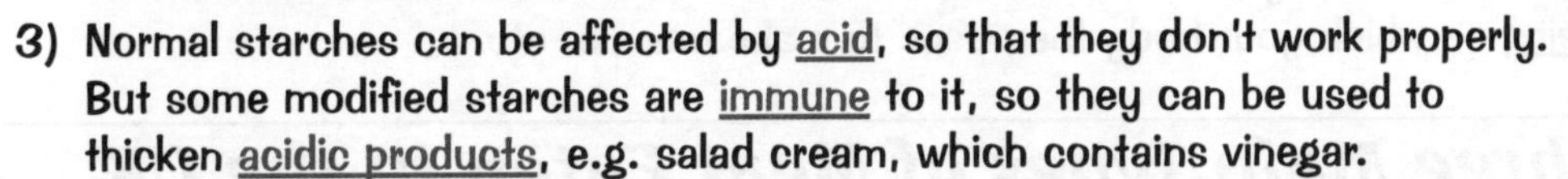

Gluten helps Bread Dough to Stretch and Rise

Bread contains lots of starch, but there are other important nutrients that give bread its properties. To make sure a loaf of bread doesn't turn out like a heavy doorstop, you need the dough to be elastic.

1) When dough made with flour is kneaded, a protein called gluten is formed.
2) To get a well-risen loaf of bread it's best to use strong bread flour because it will form more gluten than other types of flour.
3) Gluten gives dough its elasticity (stretchiness) and helps bread to rise.
4) The dough mixture contains yeast, which ferments the sugar to produce carbon dioxide — a gas.
5) The gluten stretches to hold the carbon dioxide — this is what makes bread rise.
6) When gluten reaches a high temperature it coagulates (it changes into a more solid state). The dough stays stretched to give the light, airy texture of well-risen bread.

Practice Questions

1) a) What happens when liquid is added to starch granules?
   b) In what way can this be useful when preparing food?
2) a) Briefly describe what gelatinisation means.
   b) Over what temperature range does gelatinisation occur?
3) How can starch be used to make foods thicker?
4) a) What is syneresis? How can this problem be prevented?
   b) Name two other ways that modified starches can be useful in food preparation. Give an example product for each.
5) What is the name of the protein in starch that makes bread dough elastic?

Proteins — Meat, Poultry and Fish

Meat, poultry and fish provide high-grade protein and other essential nutrients. But bacteria also like them, so you have to be really careful when buying, storing, preparing or cooking them.

Protein is Needed for Growth and Repair

1) Protein helps our bodies to build and repair muscles, tissues and organs, and helps children grow.
2) Protein is made of amino acids. Your body can make some amino acids but not others. You have to eat the amino acids that your body can't make — the essential amino acids.

Some proteins (e.g. meat, fish, eggs, milk and soya beans) contain all the essential amino acids. Other proteins (e.g. peas, lentils, nuts and most beans) only contain some of the essential amino acids, so it's important to eat a wide variety of these foods. (This is particularly true for vegans — see p35.)

3) When you eat protein, your body breaks it down into amino acids and uses these to build new proteins — which your body then uses to make muscle, etc.

There are Three Main Types of Meat Eaten in the UK...

Beef and lamb have loads of B vitamins and minerals like iron and zinc.

Pork contains lots of thiamin (vitamin B1) and niacin (B3).

1) These are called red meats (though pork is sometimes classed as white meat). They're all great sources of protein, but too much can cause problems like heart disease.
2) Meat can be tenderised to make it, well... more tender. You have to partly break down the fibres in the meat. You can do this by bashing it with a mallet, marinating it in something acidic (see p32) or cooking it really slowly (this is what makes casseroles lovely and tender).
3) Meat can dry out during cooking. To avoid this you can seal the outside of the meat (by cooking it at a high temperature for the first couple of minutes) — this keeps the juices in.

...Three Main Types of Poultry...

Chicken

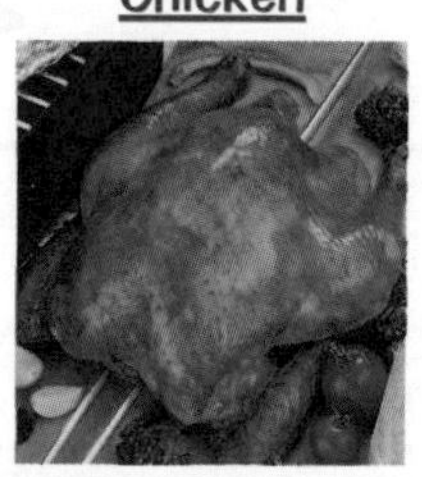

Turkey

Duck

These are white meats — though duck's often called red meat. (Zeesh, you'd think someone could just decide.)

Poultry is a good source of protein and B vitamins and is fairly low in saturated fat (especially without the skin). But it can be contaminated with salmonella bacteria, which can make you seriously ill.

That youth's no amateur — he's a pro-teen...

Sure, meat's got protein in it, but it contains other stuff as well — e.g. red meat has loads of iron, and liver has loads of vitamins. But the tastiest meat also has lots and lots of saturated fat. Shame.

Proteins — Meat, Poultry and Fish

...and Three Main Types of Fish...

Oily fish, e.g. herring, mackerel, salmon, tuna.

White fish, e.g. cod, haddock, plaice, skate.

Shellfish, e.g. crab, lobster, mussels.

Fish is very nutritious — it contains loads of vitamins, plus omega 3 oils, which are dead good for you.

There are Now Loads of Meat Replacements

1) Vegetarians don't eat meat, so they need to get their protein and other nutrients from elsewhere. Beans, lentils and nuts are all good sources of protein, as are eggs (see next page).
2) These days, there are lots of alternative proteins, such as:
   Tofu — made from soya beans.
   TVP (Textured Vegetable Protein) — also made from soya beans.
   Quorn™ — made from a mushroom-like fungus and egg white.
3) These products can be prepared in lots of ways, sometimes to look like meat or chicken:
   - TVP can be made into sausages, burgers and ready meals.
   - Tofu is usually just stir-fried, but it can also be used in desserts.
   - Quorn™ is more often used where you'd normally use chicken, and is available as chunks (e.g. for stir fries), mince (e.g. for chilli con carne) or fillets (e.g. to serve in sauces).
4) These meat replacements usually don't taste of much, so they're often flavoured. One way of doing this is by marinating them (soaking them in a mixture of things like oil, wine, vinegar and herbs) before cooking.

Practice Questions

1) What do we need proteins for?
2) List three examples of foods that contain all the essential amino acids.
3) Name two vitamins or minerals that are contained in each of the following:
   a) beef
   b) pork
4) Mary is going to cook steak for dinner. Before she fries it, she bashes it with a mallet. Explain why she does this.
5) Give one advantage and one disadvantage of eating white meats.
6) What are the three main types of fish? Give an example for each type.
7) How can someone on a vegetarian diet ensure they get the required amount of protein?
8) a) What does "marinate" mean?
   b) Why are alternative protein foods often marinated?

Proteins — Eggs

Eggs are a fabulous source of protein, and most people eat them by the bucketful. Well actually, they don't — eggs don't come in buckets. Anyway...

Eggs Have Loads of Healthy Stuff

We mainly eat hens' eggs, but goose, duck and quail eggs are also popular with some people. Anyway eggs is eggs and they're great.

NUTRITIONAL CONTENT OF EGGS

- protein — about 13%
- fat (mainly saturated) — about 10%
- vitamins A, B2 and D
- minerals, including iodine

Eggs have Loads of Uses and Functions in Cooking

Functions

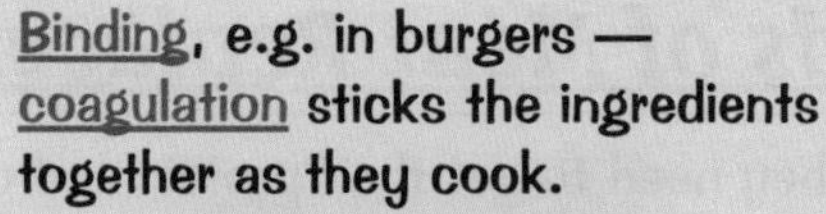

Binding, e.g. in burgers — coagulation sticks the ingredients together as they cook.

Thickening, e.g. in custard or quiche — egg white coagulates (becomes more solid) at 60°C and yolk at 70°C, so when it reaches these temperatures it sets and stays 'thickened'.

Coating or enrobing — eggs help dry ingredients like breadcrumbs to stick to food, e.g. chicken, as it's cooked.

Glazing, e.g. on bagels — brushing egg over bread gives it a glossy finish when it's cooked.

Aeration, e.g. in cakes — egg white traps air when it's beaten, because the protein stretches.

Emulsification, e.g. in salad dressings — oil and water mixed together form an emulsion (see page 38). But the emulsion usually separates after a while. Lecithin, found in egg yolks, keeps the emulsion stable (i.e. stops it separating again). That's why egg yolks are used in mayonnaise (see page 38).

Would you like a duck egg? Only if you quack it for me...

Eggs are used left, right and centre in cooking so keep going over that list of uses and functions. I love a good omelette. But watch out — they do have some problems — see the next page...

Proteins — Eggs

Chick chick chick chick chicken, lay a little egg for me... (preferably one without salmonella).

Eggs May Contain Salmonella

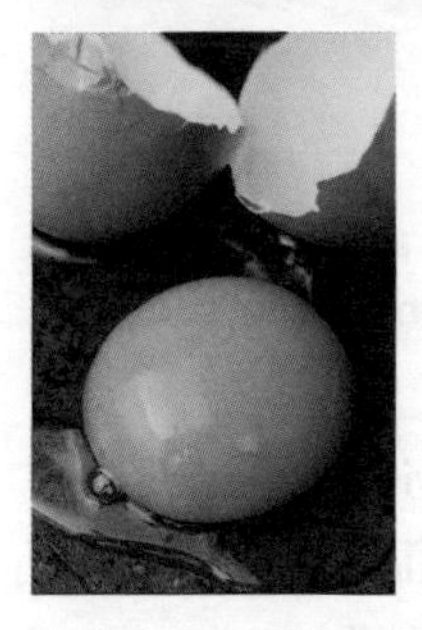

1) Raw eggs may contain the bacteria salmonella — which causes severe food poisoning. (You can also get it from chicken which hasn't been cooked properly.)
2) It's very important that eggs are cooked thoroughly so that all bacteria are destroyed.
3) You should be extra careful when cooking eggs to be eaten by pregnant women, babies and elderly or frail people.
4) Manufacturers often use dried or pasteurised egg to be on the safe side, like for mayonnaise.

EXAM TIP
If you're describing how to make a product that contains eggs, make sure you say how to ensure that they're prepared safely.

Be Careful with How You Cook Eggs

The way you cook an egg can make a lot of difference to how healthy it is.

Boiled and poached eggs are nice and healthy because they're cooked using no fat.

Scrambled eggs are healthy too — and if you do them in the microwave you don't need any fat.

A lot of people like **fried eggs** though — and these can absorb a lot of fat from the oil. It's best to use oils with unsaturated fat, and drain off as much of the oil as possible before eating them.

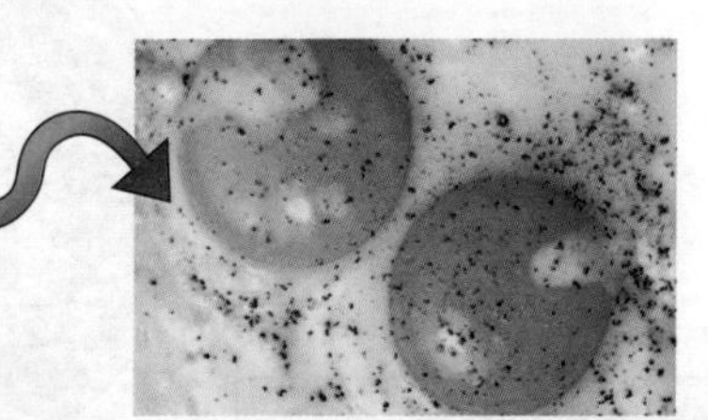

Practice Questions

1) List five nutrients contained in all eggs.
2) Explain how eggs can be used in each of the following ways, and give an example product or food for each:
   a) aeration
   b) binding
   c) thickening
3) a) What part of an egg does lecithin come from?
   b) Why is it used in mayonnaise?
4) Describe three ways you can reduce the risk of getting salmonella.
5) Why are fried eggs less healthy than boiled eggs?
6) "Humpty Dumpty's great fall could have been prevented if the King's men had been better trained." Discuss.

Fats and Oils

Ah, now we're talking — good old-fashioned fats and oils. My doctor told me to cut down, but what does he know? Waiter, two more lard rolls please...

There are Six Main Types of Fats and Oils

"Oi, hands off!"

1) Butter is made from churning cream.
2) Margarine is made from vegetable oils blended with a load of other stuff (which might include modified starch, water, emulsifiers...)
3) Lard is made from pig fat.
4) Suet is made from the fat which protects animals' vital organs.
5) Oils come from pressed seeds (e.g. rape seed, sunflower seed).
6) Low-fat spreads are emulsions of vegetable oils (usually hydrogenated — a process that makes them more solid) and water.

They're Used Loads in Pastries and Biscuits

Adding flavour — butter in shortbread and pastry makes them taste fantastic.

Shortening — rubbing fat into flour helps prevent gluten from being produced and makes pastry and biscuits 'short' — so they're a bit crumbly.

Adding colour — butter in pastry makes it golden yellow.

EXAM TIP

It's important to show the examiner that you understand both the good and bad points about fats and oils.

They're Used in Other Types of Product Too

- Cooking — deep frying (e.g. fish and chips) and shallow frying (e.g. eggs).
- Enriching — adding butter or cream to a sauce thickens it and makes it taste better.
- In emulsions — mixing together oil and water makes a thickish liquid, e.g. in vinaigrette — see page 38 for more about emulsions.

Lard... suet... dripping... Mmmm... that sounds real good...

Processed foods can contain *loads* of fat, so it's worth checking out the alternatives. We all need a certain amount of fat in our diets, although the type of fat is very important — read on...

Fats and Oils

Fats and oils get a lot of bad press — everyone's always telling you to cut down on fat. That's probably good advice, but don't go believing that they're all bad.

Fats have Some Nutritional Value

1) Fats are a concentrated source of energy.
2) Fats are a source of vitamins A, D, E and K.
3) Fats provide certain fatty acids which are essential to the structure and function of body cells.
4) The body needs a certain amount of fat to stay warm.

Unsaturated Fats OK — Saturated Fats Bad

1) Saturated fats come mainly from animal sources (e.g. meat, butter, suet, dripping, lard) and are solid or semi-solid at room temperature. They're often associated with high amounts of cholesterol — see below.

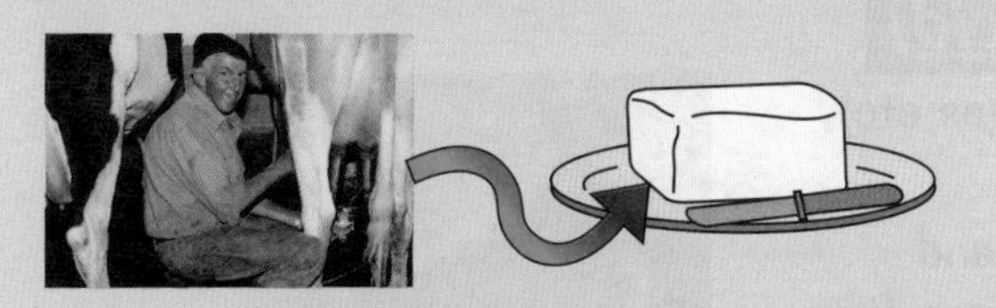

2) Unsaturated fats come mainly from vegetable sources and are usually liquid at room temperature. (Fats that are liquid at room temperature are called oils.) The main oils used in cooking are peanut, sunflower, corn, soya, rapeseed and olive oil.

Too Much Cholesterol can be Dangerous

Our bodies use fat to make cholesterol, which is an essential part of all cell membranes. It's also needed to make hormones.

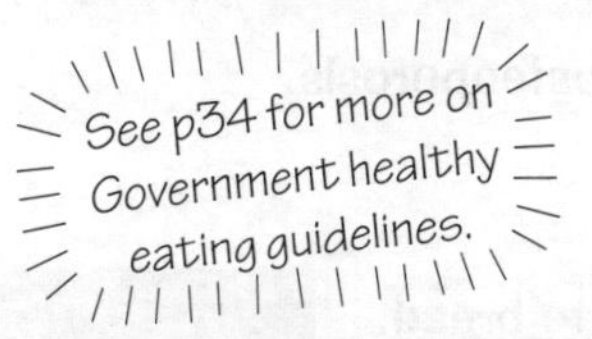

But scientists think that high cholesterol levels can increase the risk of heart disease. Most people in the UK eat more saturated fat than the Government recommends — and could probably lower their risk of heart disease by cutting down.

Practice Questions

1) List six types of fats and oils, and describe briefly how each is made.
2) a) Describe three functions of fats and oils in making pastry.
   b) Name three other ways fats and oils are used in food and cooking.
3) Explain why a diet containing no fat would be unhealthy.
4) a) What's the difference between saturated and unsaturated fats?
   b) Give two examples of each.
   c) Which is more closely linked with cholesterol — saturated or unsaturated fat?
   d) Why can having too much cholesterol in our diet be bad for our health?
5) Say "cholesterol" over and over as fast as you can until you fall over.

Vitamins and Minerals

Vitamins and minerals are essential. They help other nutrients to work and can prevent certain diseases.

We need a Balance of Different Vitamins and Minerals

Vitamin A

1) We get most of our vitamin A from retinol, which is found in liver, butter, fish oils and eggs.
2) We can also make it from carotene, which is found in orange or yellow fruit and veg and margarine.
3) Vitamin A is needed for good eyesight (especially night vision) and growth and functions of tissues.

Vitamin B Group

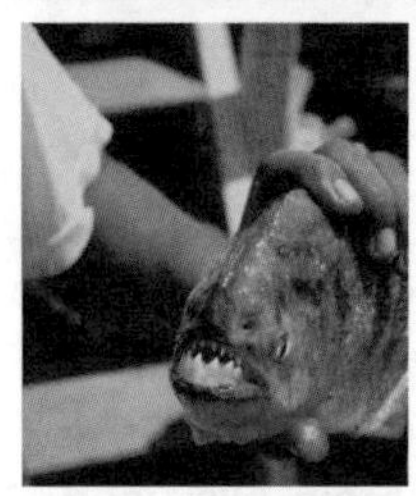

1) This is found in cereals, liver, kidney, peas, pulses, dairy produce, meat and fish.
2) B1, thiamin, helps the nervous system and the release of energy from carbohydrates.
3) B2, riboflavin, helps with the release of energy and repair of tissues.
4) B3, niacin, helps with the release of energy.
5) Folic acid is crucial for growth and important for women planning pregnancy, as low levels of folate at conception increase the risk of a baby having spina bifida.

Vitamin C (also known as Ascorbic Acid)

1) Vitamin C is found in citrus fruits (lemons, oranges etc), green vegetables, peppers and potatoes.
2) It's good for protecting the body from infection and allergies, helps in the absorption of calcium and iron from food, keeps blood vessels healthy and heals wounds.

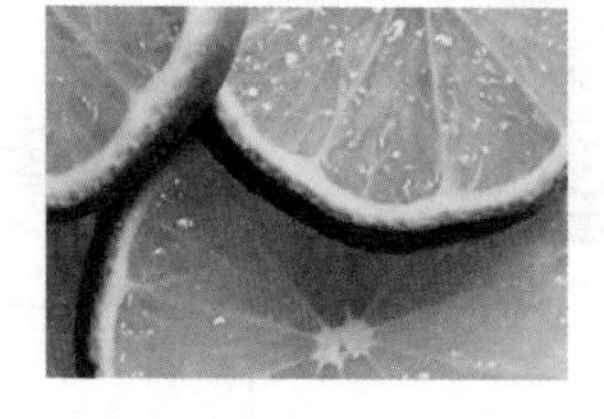

Vitamin D (also known as Calciferol)

1) Vitamin D is found in oily fish and eggs and is produced in the body when the skin is exposed to sunlight.
2) It's good because it helps the body absorb calcium.
3) A lack of it can lead to bone diseases like rickets and osteoporosis.

Calcium

1) It's found in milk, tofu, salmon, green leafy vegetables, hard water and white bread.
2) It's needed for strong bones and teeth and healthy nerves and muscles.
3) Growing children need calcium every day for strong bones and teeth. Lack of calcium in youth can lead to problems in later life (e.g. osteoporosis).

Iron

1) Iron is found in dark green vegetables (e.g. spinach) and meat (especially liver and kidney).
2) It's needed to form part of the haemoglobin which gives blood cells their red colour. Lack of iron causes a deficiency disease called anaemia.

Vitamin B Group? — my dad's got one of their records...

Loads and loads of info. And just in case you were wondering, yes, you do need to learn it all.

Vitamins and Minerals

For good health, the Government recommends we eat 5 portions of fruit and veg per day. These portions could be dried, fresh, tinned or frozen. One portion can be fruit juice (yay) — but not potatoes (boo).

Fruit and Vegetables are Dead Healthy

In a normal healthy diet, fruit and vegetables give you:

- The majority of your vitamin C intake (about 90%)
- Dietary fibre
- Vitamins A (from carotene) and B
- Iron and calcium
- Not much fat (except avocados)
- Loads of water
- Small amounts of protein.

Prepare Fruit and Veg Carefully to Keep the Good Stuff

Nutrients and flavour can easily be lost or spoilt through overcooking and poor storage.

1) Microbes (germs) in the air can make fruit and vegetables go rotten. Store them in a cool, dark place (e.g. a fridge or larder, depending on the food).
2) Prepare fruit and vegetables just before you need them — vitamin C, in particular, starts to go once the fruit and vegetables are picked, stored, cut or peeled.
3) Don't chop fruit and vegetables into small pieces — it exposes more of the surface and more nutrients are lost when they're cooked.
4) Don't leave vegetables to stand in water — vitamins B and C dissolve into the water.
5) Most of the nutrients and the fibre are found just below the skin of fruit and vegetables, so peel very thinly or use them cleaned and unpeeled if possible (like jacket potatoes).
6) Fruit and vegetables should be cooked as quickly as possible in a small amount of water. Steaming or microwaving them are the best ways to keep the nutrients.

Bananas give off a gas which makes other fruit and vegetables ripen quickly and spoil, so they need to be stored separately.

Practice Questions

1) What foods do we get vitamin A from? Why do we need it?
2) List four types of B vitamin. For each one, state why it's useful.
3) What's the main vitamin found in oranges and lemons? How does it keep us healthy?
4) How does the body get vitamin D? What happens if we don't get enough of it?
5) a) List five good sources of calcium.
   b) Look at Rupert, the dashing chap on the left. Why do our bodies need plenty of calcium?
6) Why is iron good for us? Name two good sources of it.
7) Name six nutrients found in fruit and vegetables.
8) a) List three ways in which nutrients can be lost from fruit and vegetables during preparation.
   b) For each one, describe how you can prevent this from happening.
9) Sam is 12 years old and has had several broken bones recently. He also often suffers from colds. What kind of foods would you recommend he eats more of? Explain your answer.

Additives

There are ways of improving food products so they're nicer than ever — mmm, read on...

Additives are Really Useful Substances Added to Food

1) An additive is something that's added to a food product to improve its properties.
2) Additives have loads of different uses — from improving taste to extending shelf life.
3) Some additives occur naturally and some are made artificially. Customers tend to prefer the idea of natural additives, so manufacturers try to use these where possible.
4) All additives must pass a safety test before they can be used in food. When an additive passes it gets an E number, meaning it can be used throughout the European Union, e.g. caramel colouring is E150a.

1 Preservatives

Preservatives are additives that prevent bacteria from growing — so the food lasts for longer.

EXAMPLES

- Vinegar is used to pickle foods like onions and eggs.
- Using concentrated lemon juice keep salads fresh.
- Salt is used to cure meat, e.g. ham, bacon.
- The sugar in jam preserves it.
- All of these are natural preservatives.

See p48 for how preservatives work.

2 Colourings

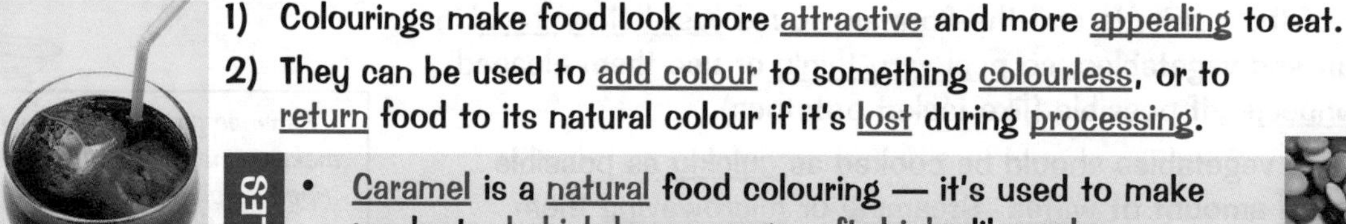

1) Colourings make food look more attractive and more appealing to eat.
2) They can be used to add colour to something colourless, or to return food to its natural colour if it's lost during processing.

EXAMPLES

- Caramel is a natural food colouring — it's used to make products darkish brown, e.g. soft drinks like cola.
- Tartrazine is an artificial food colouring — it's used to make products a yellow colour, e.g. custard powder, syrups, sweets.

3 Flavourings

Flavourings improve the taste or the aroma (smell) of a product.

EXAMPLES

- Herbs and spices are natural flavourings — they improve the taste, e.g. adding basil makes tomato-flavoured pasta sauces more tasty, and chillies add spice to a range of foods.
- Vanilla flavouring can be natural (from vanilla pods) or artificial (vanillin solution). It's used in lots of cakes and desserts, e.g. vanilla-flavoured ice-cream.
- Artificial sweetening agents, e.g. saccharin, are used in some desserts to...erm, add sweetness.
- Monosodium glutamate (MSG) is a natural flavour enhancer — it boosts the existing flavour of a product and gives it a savoury taste. MSG is added to processed foods like sauces, soups and crisps.

So can I make a chocolate-flavoured, yellow carrot then?

Unless you grow everything you eat (unlikely), you'll probably be gobbling up a fair few additives — they're just so darn useful. So make sure you know why they're useful, and learn some examples too.

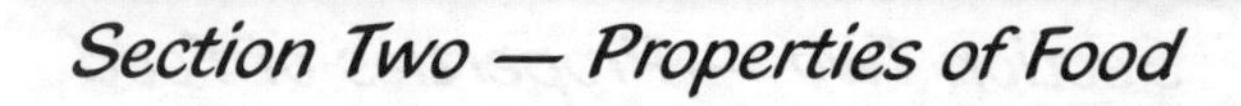

Additives

4 Emulsifiers

1) Emulsifiers are used to keep food products stable — they stop oily and watery liquids separating.
2) Lecithin is a natural emulsifier found in egg yolks — it's used in products like mayonnaise and margarine.

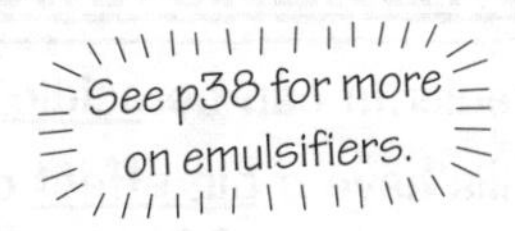

5 Setting agents

1) Setting agents are used to thicken products, so that they set as a gel (see p38).
2) Gelatine is a natural gelling agent that's extracted from animals — it's used in desserts like mousses and jellies.

This is a mousse.

This is a mouse.

6 Raising agents

1) Raising agents are used in dough and cake mixtures to aerate them. They release bubbles of gas, which expand when heated to make the mixture rise.
2) Yeast is a biological raising agent used in bread dough — yeast are microorganisms that cause fermentation, producing carbon dioxide.
3) Baking powder and bicarbonate of soda are chemical raising agents. They break down when heated, producing carbon dioxide which makes cakes rise.

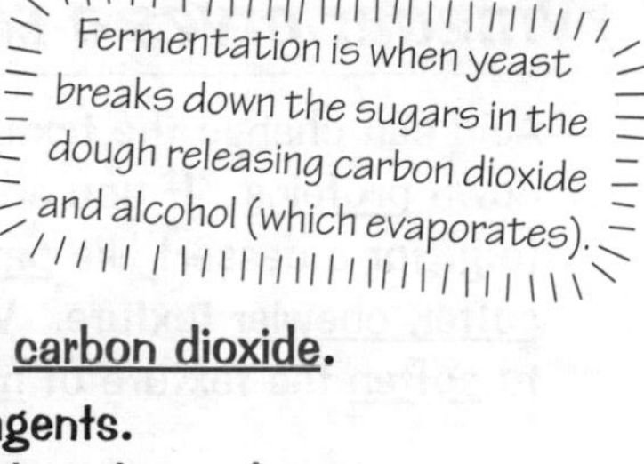

But Food Additives have Disadvantages Too

1) Some people, especially kids, are allergic to certain additives.
2) Some additives, like sugar or salt, if used in large amounts can be bad for our health.
3) They can disguise poor quality ingredients, e.g. processed meat products may not contain much meat but they can be made to taste good by using additives.
4) Although additives go through safety tests, no-one really knows the long-term health effects yet. Some people think eating additives could be linked to behavioural problems, e.g. studies are looking at whether a colouring additive called sunset yellow is linked to hyperactive behaviour in children.

Practice Questions

1) What is an additive?
2) What does it mean when an additive's been given an E number?
3) Explain why manufacturers add the following types of additive to food products:
   a) preservatives
   b) colourings
   c) setting agents
   d) emulsifiers
4) Sophie's made some sweet chilli sauce, but she isn't convinced about the taste.
   a) What could she add to make the sauce have a more savoury taste?
   b) What could she add to make it a bit sweeter?
5) a) Give an example of a biological raising agent.
   b) Give two examples of chemical raising agents.

Acids and Alkalis

Chemistry — aaaaaaargh... No wait, there are pictures of food, so it must be the right subject. Phew.

Acids and Alkalis Change the Properties of Foods

1) Food and ingredients can be acidic, neutral or alkaline.
2) Acids and alkalis have a big effect on the flavour, texture and appearance of foods.
3) So you need to know the pH of your ingredients to know how your final product will turn out.

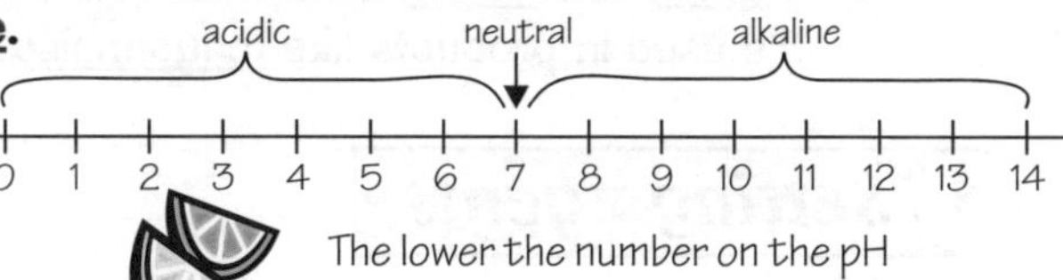

The lower the number on the pH scale, the more acidic something is. Lemon juice has a pH of about 2.

Acids have Loads of Different Uses...

Acidic foods include citrus fruits, lemon juice (citric acid), vinegar (acetic acid) and vitamin C (ascorbic acid). They have a sharp, sour taste.

1 Vinegar gives a softer texture

Acid can change the texture of foods by partly breaking down proteins. If you add vinegar when making meringue (e.g. for a dessert like pavlova) it gives the meringue a softer, chewier texture. Vinegar is also used in marinades to soften the texture of meat — this is called tenderising.

2 Lemon juice prevents enzymic browning

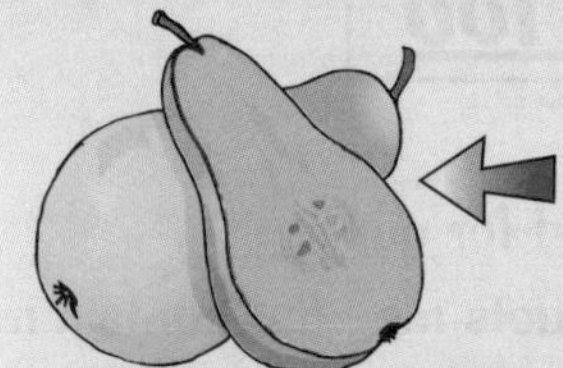

When you slice fruits (e.g. pears), the inside surfaces of the fruit react with oxygen in the air — the reaction is called enzymic browning and it turns the fruit brown.

But if you dip your slices of fruit into lemon juice straight away, the acidic conditions stop enzymic browning. The colour of the fruit is retained, which is really useful, e.g. for the nice appearance of fruit salads.

3 Lactic acid fermentation produces yogurts

Milk turns sour when the bacteria it contains break down sugars in the milk into lactic acid. In yogurt-making, lactic acid acts on the proteins in milk to thicken it. The lactic acid gives yogurt its slightly sour taste.

4 Acids add flavour

Acids are added to give a sharp flavour, e.g. vinegar is often used in salad dressings.

5 Acids help preserve foods

The acidic conditions help to preserve foods because bacteria can't grow (see p49).

Acids and alkalis — sour and bitter — mmm....

Hmm, I don't know about you but adding vinegar to a meringue just doesn't seem right somehow. That's the thing with chemistry — you never know if you'll end up with a masterpiece or a soggy mess...

Acids and Alkalis

Alkalis have a Couple of Uses...

Foods like bicarbonate of soda and cornflour are alkaline.
They have a fairly unpleasant, bitter taste.

1) Bicarbonate of soda acts as a raising agent

Bicarbonate of soda breaks down to produce carbon dioxide when it's heated. The carbon dioxide bubbles expand and make mixtures rise.

You need to use bicarbonate of soda together with a strong flavour, to mask the unpleasant taste it leaves — so it's used in things like gingerbread and chocolate cake.

2) Cornflour gives a thicker texture

Cornflour is used in lots of products to thicken them. For example, you add cornflour to thicken the filling in good old lemon meringue pie.

EXAM TIP
Make sure you know some specific examples of what acids and alkalis are used for in food production.

Practice Questions

1) Acids and alkalis change the flavour of foods.
   What else might they change?
2) What kind of flavour do strongly acidic foods have?
3) What do strongly alkaline foods taste like?
4) Kendra is making a lemon meringue pie.
   a) What could she add to her meringue to give it a softer texture?
   b) How could she make the lemon filling a bit thicker?
5) Roberto and Mario are about to prepare a fruit salad.
   It won't be served till later, but they want it to look really fresh.
   a) Name an acid or an alkali that you would recommend they use in the fruit salad.
   b) Explain how your recommended ingredient would help.
6) a) Describe a common function of bicarbonate of soda.
   b) Name two foods that are often made using bicarbonate of soda.

Healthy Eating

The Government issues guidelines on healthy eating. Crunch some lettuce while you read all about it.

Use the Eatwell Plate to Check your Diet is Right

The eatwell plate is an easy way of showing how much or little of each food group you should eat:

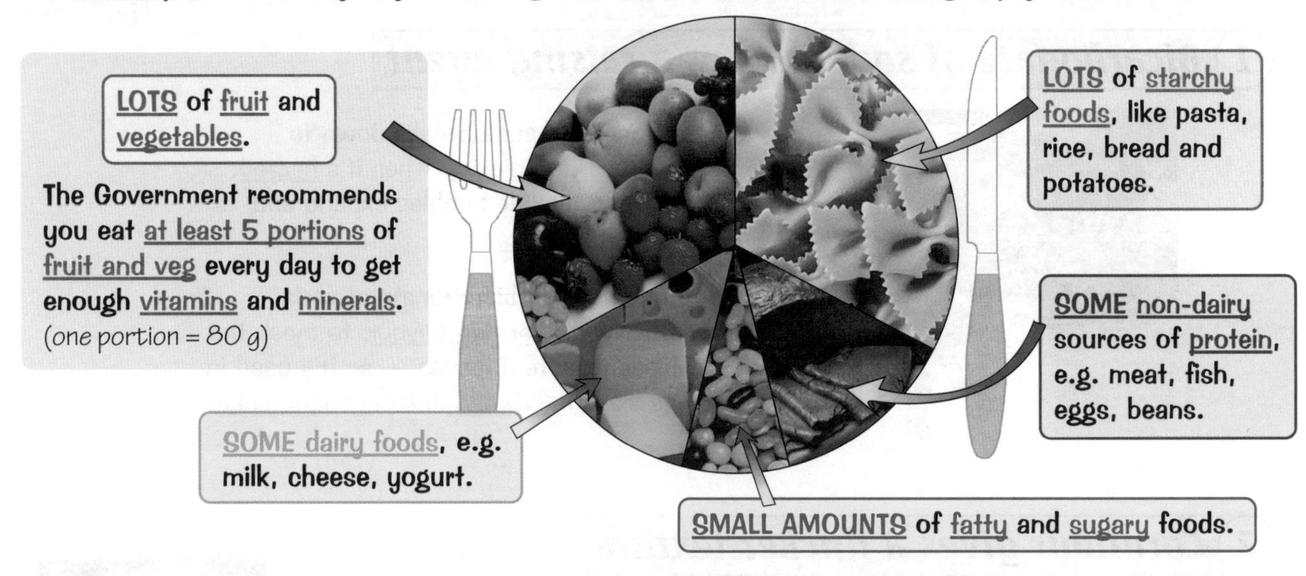

You Need Certain Amounts of Each Nutrient

Many food labels show you how much of various nutrients the product contains. They often refer to Guideline Daily Amounts (GDAs) or Recommended Daily Amounts (RDAs) — this is how much of each nutrient and how much energy an average adult needs each day.

Labels usually show how much protein, carbohydrate, fat and dietary fibre the product contains.

The amount of each nutrient is sometimes shown as a percentage of the GDA as well.

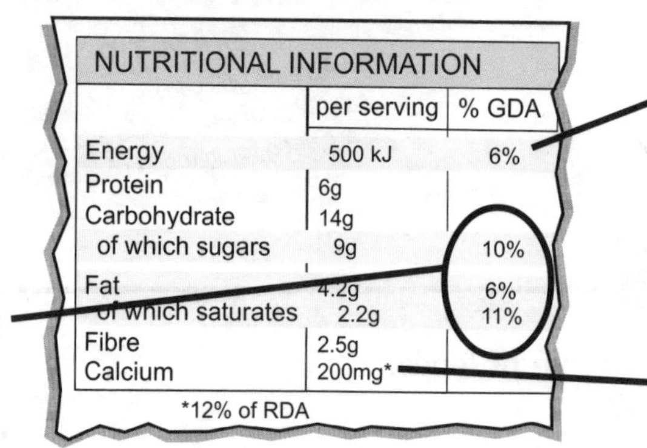

NUTRITIONAL INFORMATION	per serving	% GDA
Energy	500 kJ	6%
Protein	6g	
Carbohydrate	14g	
of which sugars	9g	10%
Fat	4.2g	6%
of which saturates	2.2g	11%
Fibre	2.5g	
Calcium	200mg*	

*12% of RDA

One serving of this product contains 6% of the daily energy requirement.

RDAs are used for vitamins and minerals. One serving of this product contains 12% of the recommended daily calcium intake.

A diet with not enough or too much of certain nutrients can cause health problems:

Nutrient deficiencies

1) Not getting enough vitamins or minerals can lead to many health problems, see p28.
2) Not eating enough protein leads to restricted growth in children, and also leads to muscle wastage.

Nutrient excesses

1) Eating too much fat can make you overweight or obese, which can lead to heart problems and cancer.
2) Eating too much sugar can lead to obesity, Type 2 diabetes and tooth decay.
3) Too much salt can increase blood pressure, meaning a bigger risk of heart disease and stroke.

An eatwell plate — I prefer a Bakewell myself...

You can check how healthy your diet is by keeping a food diary of everything you eat, and comparing this to the guidelines. The important thing is to get a balanced diet over a day or so. And to revise.

Healthy Eating

Different Groups have Different Dietary Needs

Some people can't or won't eat some foods. When you're designing a product, you need to think about the ingredients you'll be using and whether they'll be suitable for different groups of people.

VEGETARIANS don't eat meat or fish.

1) Vegans don't eat any animal products, e.g. they won't eat milk or cheese.
2) Vegetarians and vegans need to get protein and vitamins from foods like nuts, beans and lentils or from meat replacements (see p23).

People with **COELIAC DISEASE** can't eat a protein called gluten, found in wheat, rye and barley.

1) So coeliacs can't eat normal bread or pasta.
2) They have to get starch and fibre from other foods, e.g. rice and potatoes, or from gluten-free alternatives, e.g. gluten-free bread.

People who are **LACTOSE INTOLERANT** can't digest lactose, which is a sugar found in milk.

1) So they need to avoid cow's milk and many dairy products, and any products that lactose is added to, e.g. peanut butter.
2) Dairy products are an important source of calcium for most people. Lactose intolerant people have to get calcium from foods like green leafy vegetables, salmon and white bread.

1) People who are overweight need to eat a **CALORIE-CONTROLLED** diet.
2) Fat and sugar provide a lot of calories without filling you up. The recommended method to lose weight is to get your energy from starchy foods instead (and to take a bit more exercise).

1) People with **NUT ALLERGIES** need to avoid products that contain nuts or have traces of nuts.
2) If you're designing a product containing nuts, consider putting a warning label on the packaging.

DIABETICS can't control their blood sugar levels.

1) They need to avoid eating very sugary foods.
2) Diabetics are advised to eat plenty of starchy foods, which release energy slowly, to avoid having very high or very low blood sugar levels.

Practice Questions

1) List the five major food groups on the eatwell plate.
2) How could you check how much of your daily requirement of fat is in a food product you're buying?
3) Look at Peter's food diary. Use the food diary to describe how well Peter meets the healthy eating guidelines set out in the eatwell plate.

   Breakfast — wholemeal toast & jam
   Snack — chocolate bar
   Lunch — egg & cheese sandwich, crisps, chocolate, yogurt
   Dinner — chicken curry & rice
   Dessert — cake

4) a) Explain how eating too little protein can be bad for you.
   b) Explain how eating too much sugar can be bad for you.
5) Susie is hosting a dinner party and plans to serve beef lasagne.
   a) One of her friends is vegetarian. Suggest how Susie could make her a suitable lasagne.
   b) One of her friends is a coeliac. Why might this be a problem for Susie and how could she alter her lasagne to make it suitable?

New Technology

Get scientists involved in food technology and there's no end to what you can do...

There are New Production Methods, Foods and Packaging

1) Producers use new technologies to meet consumer demands, e.g. for food that lasts longer.
2) New methods of producing food all year round include using huge greenhouses called biodomes.
3) New ingredients and foods include meat substitutes like TVP and tofu, modified starch (see p21), genetically modified foods and functional foods (see below).
4) New packaging technology includes breathable packaging for fruits, and packaging with more protection against moisture and bacteria — see page 58 for more.

Genetically Modified Foods have Altered Genes

1) A genetically modified (GM) food is one that's had its genes altered to give it useful characteristics. *GM plants are produced by inserting a desirable gene from another plant, an animal or a bacteria into the plant you want to improve. You plant modified seeds and up comes your GM crop.*
2) For example, you can get GM maize that's pest-resistant. The farmer gets a bigger yield of maize because less of the crop is eaten or damaged by pests.

GM foods have advantages...

1) Crops can be made to grow quickly.
2) Producers can get a higher yield of crops for the same amount of seed and fertiliser.
3) This makes food cheaper to produce so it's also cheaper for the consumer to buy.
4) Crops can be altered to have a longer shelf life — so less food is wasted.
5) Crops can be made to ripen earlier than normal, so fresh foods can be available for consumers earlier in the year.

...and disadvantages

1) GM foods haven't been around for long — so their long-term health effects aren't known.
2) There are concerns that modified genes could get out into the wider environment and cause problems, e.g. the weedkiller resistance gene could be transferred to a weed, making it a 'superweed'.
3) GM producers can't sell their food everywhere — the European Union (EU) restricts the import of some GM foods.

Consumers and the EU have Safety Concerns

Some people believe that we shouldn't mess about with genes because it's not natural. To help consumers make an informed choice, the European Union (EU) has rules:

1) All GM foods must undergo strict safety assessments and they can only be sold if they're found to have no health risks.
2) All foods that are GM or contain more than 1% GM ingredients must be clearly labelled.

Altering genes — easy, just turn up the trouser legs...

New technology can help food producers and consumers... but not everyone's convinced that the benefits outweigh the risks. Make sure you know the pros and cons of GM foods and what the EU says.

New Technology

Functional Foods have Added Health Benefits

"...and an extra large pizza with omega-3 topping please..."

A functional food is one that's has been artificially modified to provide a particular health benefit, on top of its normal nutritional value. For example:

- Some fruit juices have calcium (which is important for healthy bones) added to them.
- Eggs containing high levels of the fatty acid omega-3 (which may reduce your risk of heart disease and cancer) can be produced by feeding hens a diet rich in omega-3.
- Some functional foods are made by genetic modification, e.g. Golden Rice is rice that's been genetically modified to contain carotene (which provides vitamin A, important for good eyesight).

They solve some problems...

1) Functional foods are an easy way of providing better nutrition for people who have a poor diet.
2) People who can't eat (or don't like) certain foods can get the 'missing' nutrients from functional foods.
3) Foods like Golden Rice could help solve some health problems caused by malnutrition in poor countries.

...but not all

1) People still need to eat a varied diet and exercise to be healthy — they can't rely on just eating functional foods.
2) Functional foods don't always provide all of the nutrient you'd need. E.g. it might be difficult for people to eat loads of Golden Rice every day to get enough vitamin A.
3) They don't tackle the actual causes of malnutrition in poor countries.

But Some Consumers are Worried

Many consumers are concerned about what's in food and they don't know whether to believe everything manufacturers tell them.

1) If manufacturers make health claims for their foods, e.g. 'helps to maintain a healthy heart', then the relevant ingredients must be clearly labelled and the nutritional information must be on the label (see page 56 for more on labelling laws).
2) Health claims mustn't mislead consumers, and must be backed up by scientific evidence.

Practice Questions

1) What is a genetically modified (GM) food?
2) How does growing a GM crop that's resistant to pests help farmers?
3) a) Describe three benefits that GM foods can bring.
   b) Give two potential disadvantages of GM foods.
4) How does the European Union (EU) help consumers make informed choices about GM food?
5) a) What is a functional food?
   b) Describe two ways functional foods can be made.
6) A label on a carton of orange juice says it 'helps to maintain healthy bones'.
   a) What does the manufacturer need to put on the label to back up this claim?
   b) What functional ingredient would you expect to see added to the orange juice?

Combining Ingredients

How a product turns out depends on the ingredients you use and how they react with each other.

Solution — a Solid is Dissolved in a Liquid

sugar + water → a solution

1) A solution forms when solid ingredients completely dissolve in a liquid, e.g. sugar dissolves in water to make a solution.
2) You can't tell the separate ingredients apart once they've formed a solution.

flour and water suspension

Suspension — a Solid is Held in a Liquid

1) A suspension forms when solid ingredients are added to a liquid but don't dissolve, e.g. flour mixed with water forms a cloudy suspension.
2) If you don't stir the mixture, the solid usually sinks to the bottom.
3) If you stir and heat up a starchy suspension, it'll thicken into a sauce (see p20).

Emulsion — Oil and Watery Stuff Mixed Together

1) An emulsion is formed when oily and watery liquids are mixed together and the droplets of one spread out through the other — they usually separate unless you keep shaking or stirring them.
2) Emulsions need an emulsifier to stop the oil separating from the liquid.
3) There's a natural emulsifier in egg yolks — it's called lecithin.
4) Egg yolks are used as emulsifiers in foods like margarine to hold together the oil and the liquid.
5) Many types of salad dressings are emulsions, e.g:

- Mayonnaise is a stable emulsion of egg yolk, oil and vinegar (often with other flavourings).
- Vinaigrette is an emulsion of oil and vinegar. It's unstable — it separates if you don't shake it.

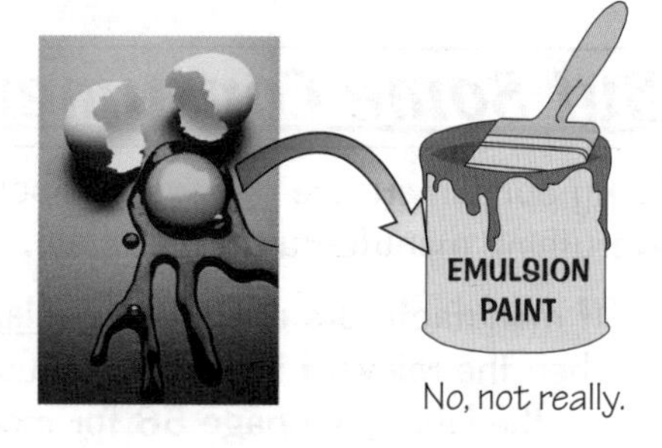

No, not really.

Gel — a Small Amount of Solid Sets a Lot of Liquid

1) A gel is like a thick solution, in between a liquid and a solid. (Well, not exactly... but you don't need to know the full chemistry explanation.)

2) Some cold desserts are gels, e.g. jellies, mousses, cheesecakes.
3) Only a small amount of solid ingredient is needed to set a lot of liquid, e.g. a small amount of gelatine can set a lot of water to form jelly.
4) There's a natural gelling agent in some fruits — it's called pectin. Pectin is released from these fruits during cooking and it helps foods like jams to set.

I need to find a solution soon — I can't take the suspension...

The key to making loads of food products is to know what happens when you combine ingredients in different ways. Make sure you learn an example of a solution, a suspension, an emulsion and a gel.

Combining Ingredients

You can Change the Taste of your Food Product...

Food products are made to meet specific criteria (see p12). You can make your food product exactly how you want it (the right colour, texture, taste, etc.) by doing these things:

You can change the ingredients

To make a cake look darker you could swap white flour for wholemeal flour. Or to give it a different flavour you could vanilla essence or lemon zest.

You can change the proportion of ingredients

To make a cake taste nuttier you could, er, add more nuts. Or to make it more moist you could add more eggs to the mixture.

You can change the way you combine the ingredients

To make a cake more light and fluffy you could beat the egg whites for longer. If your cake's a bit too heavy you could try folding the flour into the mixture instead of beating it.

You need to accurately measure and record any changes you make to your product — so you can make it exactly the same next time. This is really important when making your product on a large scale — any measuring errors could be expensive and waste time if you make a rubbish batch or run out of ingredients. Use things like measuring spoons, measuring jugs and electronic scales to measure everything accurately.

...and you can Change its Nutritional Value

If you want to change the nutritional value of your food product (to meet specific criteria) then you need to change the ingredients or the proportions of ingredients.

1) Low-sugar cakes and biscuits — you could experiment using less sugar to make a cake or biscuits. You might have to swap sugar for another sweet ingredient, e.g. honey or fruit. But you'll have to experiment to get the proportions and the cooking time right.
2) Low-fat pastry — you could try using less fat in pastry, e.g. use less butter, but you'd have to make sure the texture of the pastry was still suitable for the product you were making.
3) Gluten-free bread — you could make bread using gluten-free flour, but the texture would be very heavy without any gluten to make the dough elastic. To avoid this, you could add xanthan gum to the dough — this makes it 'stickier' and gives the final product a much better texture.
4) Low-salt sauces — you could make a sauce with very little salt — but you might have to give it more flavour some other way, e.g. use less salt in tomato sauce but add some basil instead.

Practice Questions

1) What is an emulsion?
2) Name one example of:
   a) a natural emulsifier
   b) a gel
3) Explain the difference between a solution and a suspension.
4) Jane owns a bakery. She wants to make a low-fat version of her apple pie but she doesn't want to use different ingredients.
   a) Give two examples of how Jane could make her new version of apple pie.
   b) Suggest what problems might occur when Jane first tries making this new version.

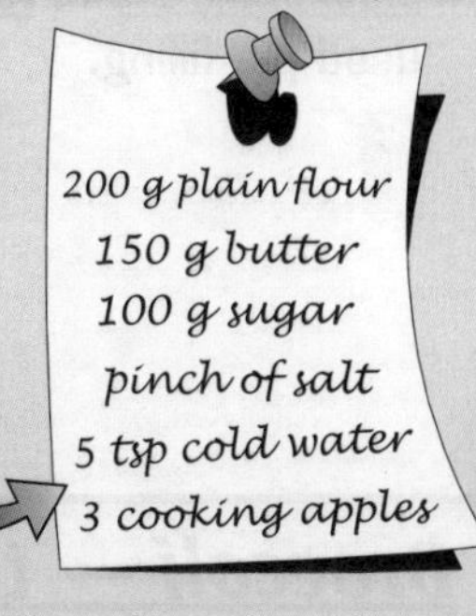

Standard Food Components

In industry, manufacturers don't always make their products from scratch...

Standard Food Components are Ready-Made Ingredients

1) Manufacturers can buy in food parts that have already been made by other manufacturers, e.g. pizza bases, fillings. These ingredients are called standard food components.
2) Standard food components are really useful — they cut out a lot of time and work.
3) It's not just manufacturers — catering businesses and people cooking at home use standard food components too. Here are some examples:

Pastry, Pizza Bases and Cake Mixes

Standard food components include things like pizza bases, chilled and frozen pastry, cake mixes and bread mixes. It's much quicker to start off with a ready-made component than to make it yourself — then you can adapt it as you need, e.g. you can put your own fillings into pies but start off with ready-made pastry.

EXAM TIP
You could get marks just for naming some standard components that might be used to make a product.

Fillings and Sauces

Ready-made fillings and sauces save you the bother of having to prepare all the separate ingredients. They also have a longer shelf-life than fresh products and can be used at any time of year, not just when the fresh products are in season. For example, you could make a blackberry pie in January if you used pie filling.

Icing and Marzipan

Ready-to-roll icing and marzipan are easy ways to decorate products without having to prepare everything yourself. For example, a cake business might order in ready-made marzipan in various colours, but cut and shape it themselves to make the decorations they need.

Using icing to decorate a cake is an example of a finishing technique.

Broccoli — the standard food component used by all mums...

If you can stop drooling over cake for long enough to learn this, you'll see standard food components are dead useful. Your basic ingredients come ready-made — ace. If only exams came ready-answered.

Standard Food Components

Using Standard Food Components has Advantages...

1) It saves time — you don't have to bother preparing the basic ingredients.
2) It saves money — manufacturers can often buy standard components frozen, in bulk, which is more cost-effective than buying fresh ingredients separately and making the components themselves.
3) Less machinery and less specialist equipment is needed, which also saves money.
4) Fewer specialist skills are needed by staff because the standard components are ready to use.
5) Food preparation is safer and more hygienic — especially if high-risk products like chicken, eggs or soiled vegetables are stored and prepared somewhere else.
6) The product is more likely to be consistent — standard food components are quality-controlled so they all have the same flavour, texture, weight, shape, colour, etc.

The product is always the same.

...and Disadvantages

The production line can be held up.

1) You can't pick and choose exactly what you want, e.g. you can't get the ready-made pastry made a tiny bit sweeter.
2) It's not always reliable — late deliveries from the supplier will hold up the production line.
3) The product may not be as tasty as one made with fresh ingredients.
4) Extra space might be needed to store the standard food components if you've bought them in bulk.
5) There's extra packaging and transport involved, so it might be bad for the environment.

Practice Questions

1) Give two examples of standard food components you might use when:
   a) decorating a cake
   b) making a pizza
2) A pie manufacturer chooses to buy chicken filling as a standard food component.
   a) How does this make food preparation safer and more hygienic for the pie manufacturer?
   b) Suggest another standard food component the manufacturer might use and explain why.
   c) Give another advantage for the manufacturer of using standard food components in their product.

3) Give two reasons why manufacturers might choose not to use standard food components.
4) Billy buys a hot dog with freshly fried onions, tomato ketchup and mustard at a food fair. Suggest three standard food components that may have been used to make his snack.

Scale of Production

Manufacturers use different types of production depending on how many of a product they're making.

One-Off Production — Every Product's Unique

1) This is where you make a single product (it's also called 'job production').
2) Every product's made differently to meet a specific request, e.g. a wedding cake.
3) Every product needs an individual recipe and an individual method.
4) Experienced workers with specialist skills are needed.
5) The products are high quality but they take a lot of time and cost a lot.

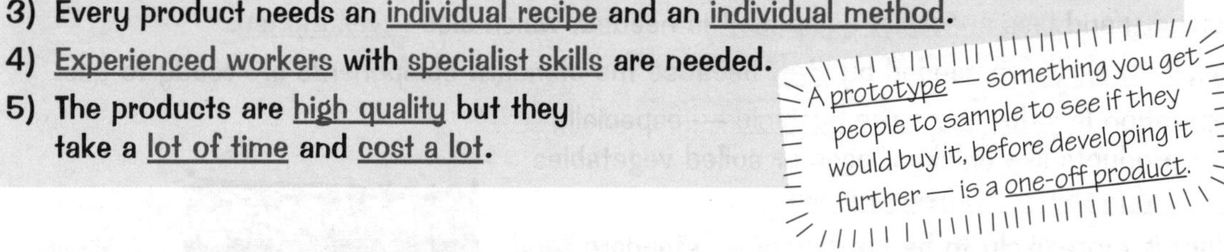

A prototype — something you get people to sample to see if they would buy it, before developing it further — is a one-off product.

Batch Production — Specified Quantities of a Product

1) This is where you make lots of your product in one go — each load you make is called a batch.
2) Every batch is made to meet specific requests from retailers, e.g. 100 chicken pies.
3) You can change batches to make another similar product, e.g. 500 steak pies.
4) But machines need to be cleaned between batches — this 'down time' is unproductive. Staff and machines need to be flexible so batches can be changed quickly, to avoid losing too much money.
5) Batch production is quicker than one-off production and it's a bit cheaper.

Mass Production — Large Quantities of a Product

1) This is where you make large numbers of a product that sells well, e.g. a loaf of sliced bread.
2) The product's made using a production line — it passes through various stages of production. Products are made very quickly so they're cheap.
3) Machines are used at some of the stages so fewer workers are needed.
4) But to make a new product you need to change the production line — this can take a long time and this unproductive time costs money.

Continuous Flow — Non-Stop Production 24hrs/day

1) This is where you make a product all the time, with no interruptions. It's basically non-stop mass production, with a production line using expensive, specialised equipment.
2) It's used for products that are sold regularly and in large numbers, e.g. baked beans.
3) It'd cost too much to keep turning equipment off and then re-starting it — so everything runs all the time. This keeps production costs really low.
4) But if anything goes wrong it takes time to get it going again, and unproductive time costs money.

A continuous flow of baked beans may produce side effects...

As usual, it's all about money. It's much cheaper for industries to produce something in huge numbers than one at a time — but it only works if the products needed are all the same and if they sell really well.

Scale of Production

CAD Helps to Design Products...

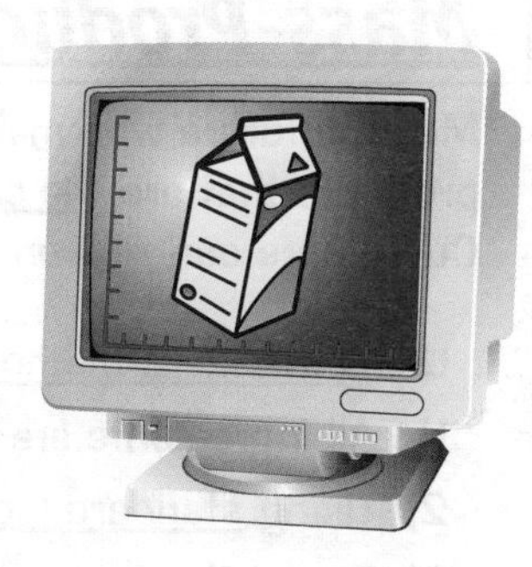

1) This is where computers are used to help design a product.
2) You can use computer-aided design (CAD) to produce models of the product and its packaging in 2D and 3D — so you can view them from any angle.
3) Once the product's been drawn on screen, you can easily recalculate values and change the design until you're happy. CAD is more accurate and much quicker than drawing and re-drawing your designs on paper.
4) CAD is really useful to calculate things like your product's nutritional value (see page 11) portion size, shelf-life and what it'll cost to make.

...and CAM Helps to Manufacture Them

Computers are used in the manufacturing process too — it's called computer-aided manufacture (CAM). Computers control some or all of the production stages, e.g. they're used to weigh out the correct amount of each ingredient, set the correct oven temperature and cooking time, etc. The whole production process is overseen by someone who keeps a close eye on everything.

Production costs are lower because fewer staff are needed.

CAM is more accurate, e.g. ingredients are weighed precisely — there's less human error.

Because machines are controlled by computers, staff don't need to go near sharp blades.

It can be quicker too — computers can make the production process more efficient.

Staff don't need to handle the food as much, making production more hygienic.

Products are more consistent — they're exactly the same each time.

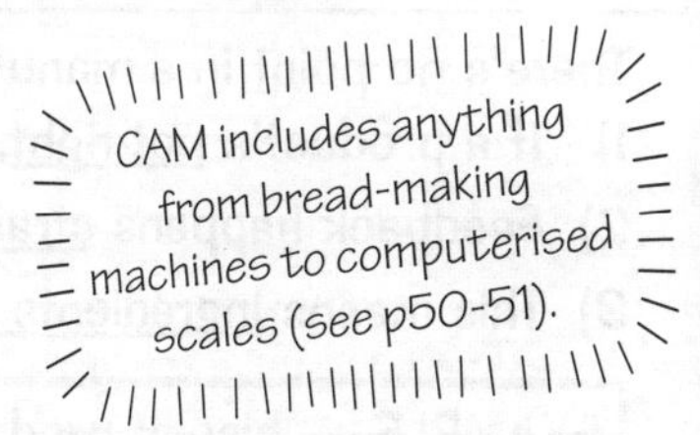

Practice Questions

1) What is mass production?
2) What does CAM stand for?
3) Describe how using CAD helps a manufacturer to design their product.
4) A cafe sells a range of sandwiches and usually sells about 1000 sandwiches per day.
   a) Suggest what method of sandwich production would most suit the cafe and explain why.
   b) A customer wants to order a type of sandwich that isn't on the cafe's menu, so the owner agrees to make it for him. What is this method of production called?
5) A manufacturer decides to produce a breakfast cereal using continuous flow.
   a) What is continuous flow?
   b) Why might the manufacturer choose this method of production?
   c) Give one disadvantage of continuous flow.
   d) The cereal is produced using CAM. Give two advantages for the manufacturer of using CAM.

Quality Control

If a product is high quality, customers are more likely to buy it again.

Mass-Produced Products need to be Consistent

Manufacturers who make products on a large scale aim to produce consistent products — products that are the same every time, e.g. they have the same taste, colour, portion size, etc. Customers can rely on the product being just like the one they liked before.

Using standard methods and equipment helps to produce consistent products, e.g:

1) All ingredients are weighed using accurate electronic scales so they're a consistent weight.
2) Using standard moulds, templates and cutting devices produces a consistent size and shape.
3) To get the flavour and texture consistent, standard food components can be used (see p40).
4) Using identical ingredients, cooking times and temperatures gives a consistent colour.

Products are Checked by Quality Control

Manufacturers set standards that their product must meet and they check to make sure these standards are being met — this is called quality control. Checks are made at every stage of production and the final product is checked too.

1) Visual checks
   - The colour of the product is checked against a standard colour.
   - The packaging is checked to make sure it's not damaged and all the labels are clearly printed.
2) Testing
   - The taste is tested at the end, to make sure it's exactly what the manufacturer wants.
   - The size, thickness and pH of the product may also be tested.

Any Problems are Fed Back Straight Away

There's no point in a manufacturer doing all this checking unless any problems are then corrected.

1) If a product's not right, the problem is relayed back to the factory floor — this is called feedback.
2) Feedback happens straight away so the problem can be fixed quickly.
3) This means ingredients aren't wasted — so the manufacturer doesn't waste time and money.

EXAMPLE — biscuit production

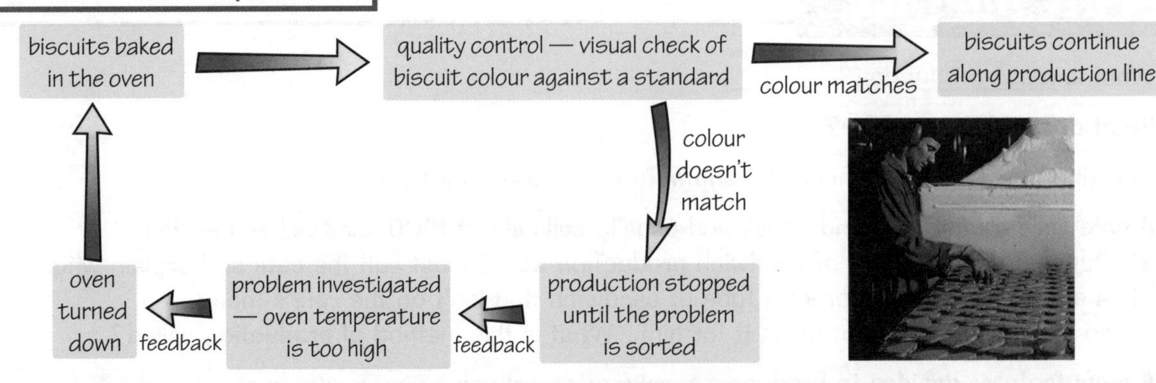

CGP has quality control — you should see the gags we reject...

It makes sense to check that a product's right before you spend tons of money making loads more. Quality control is about checking you're meeting standards and doing something about it if you're not.

Quality Control

Manufacturers Need to Avoid Contamination

Manufacturers need to make sure that their products won't harm the consumer. So they identify potential problems and put controls in place to prevent food being contaminated before it reaches the consumer.

There are three types of contamination that food manufacturers look out for:

BIOLOGICAL contamination

1) The product could become contaminated by bacteria, especially if it contains high-risk foods (see p46). E.g. there's a risk that eggs could carry salmonella.
2) To control this risk, random samples of eggs would be tested for salmonella near the beginning of the production process. You could also take samples of the end product, e.g. quiche, to be extra cautious.
3) There's loads more about preventing biological contamination on pages 46 to 49.

I couldn't find a photo of salmonella bacteria, so here's a good-looking young chap on a bike instead. Much nicer anyway.

CHEMICAL contamination

1) The product could become contaminated by, say, cleaning fluids during storage or processing.
2) To control this risk, cleaning products should be stored away from food and the final product should be tested to check there's no contamination.

PHYSICAL contamination

1) The product could become contaminated by physical objects, e.g. bits of jewellery, chipped nail varnish, hair, insects, etc.
2) To control these risks, workers wear overalls and hairnets, with no jewellery or nail varnish allowed, and food is kept covered as much as possible.

Practice Questions

1) What is a consistent product?
2) What is meant by quality control?
3) Why is it important for feedback to happen straight away?
4) A worker checks that the flapjacks passing him on the conveyor belt are the correct size. He notices that some are too small. Explain what should happen in the feedback process to fix this problem.
5) A manufacturer mass-produces a chicken tikka masala ready-meal.
   a) Describe how the manufacturer could use quality control to ensure the product is of a high standard.
   b) Give an example of possible biological contamination during the manufacturing process.
   c) How could the risk of this contamination be controlled?

Food Contamination and Bacteria

If people eat food that's contaminated by biological, chemical or physical hazards they could become very ill. So you have to handle food safely and hygienically.

Bacteria are the Main Cause of Food Poisoning

1) The symptoms of food poisoning include sickness, diarrhoea, stomach cramps and fever. In extreme cases, especially where people are old or vulnerable, it can lead to death.
2) The main cause of food poisoning is eating food (or drinking water) that's contaminated by bacteria. Bacteria are found in air, water, soil, people, animals — pretty much everywhere, really.
3) You can't see bacteria — they're so small you've got to use a microscope to spot them.
4) They often don't make the food look, taste or smell any different — so it's hard to know they're there.
5) Bacteria like conditions where they can multiply very quickly. These include:
   - moisture
   - warmth
   - neutral pH

Food poisoning can also be caused by chemical or physical contamination — see p45.

Bacteria Grow Fastest in High-Risk Foods

High-risk foods are foods that bacteria grow quickly in, because they're moist and high in protein. High-risk foods include:

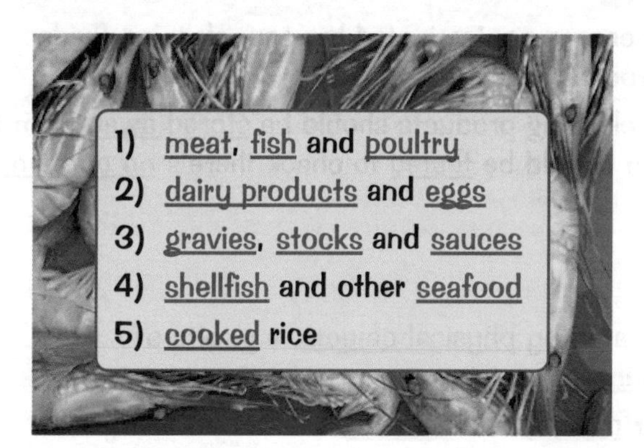

1) meat, fish and poultry
2) dairy products and eggs
3) gravies, stocks and sauces
4) shellfish and other seafood
5) cooked rice

EXAM TIP
You could get extra marks for saying why certain foods are high risk (because of their moisture and protein content).

High-risk foods have a short shelf life — you can't keep them for long, or the bacteria multiply to dangerous levels.

Avoid Cross-Contamination

When working with food, it's really easy to pass bacteria from raw food to work surfaces, equipment and your hands. Bacteria are then easily transferred to other food — this is called cross-contamination.

1) When you're preparing raw meat, keep the knives and the chopping boards you use separate from anything else you're preparing.
2) Always wash your hands thoroughly after handling raw meat.
3) Never put raw meat and cooked meat together.
4) Don't let the blood and juices of raw meat drip onto other food — always store raw meat on the bottom shelf in the fridge and keep it covered.

Baked bean curry — that's a high-risk food (to others)...

Knowing all this stuff will help you through your GCSE and it'll save your stomach loads of grief — so it must be worth it. Learn the examples of high-risk foods and how to use them safely.

Food Contamination and Bacteria

Follow Safety and Hygiene Procedures at Every Step

PURCHASING FOOD

- Always buy food from a reputable supplier so you know it's good quality.
- Take note of the use by date and make sure you can use it before this date.
- Check food carefully, e.g. make sure it hasn't been squashed or gone mouldy, check the packaging isn't damaged and the seal is still intact.

- Always follow the storage instructions — especially about temperature.
- Use old purchases before they go out of date.
- Keep food sealed or covered up.

PREPARING FOOD

- Follow personal hygiene procedures — wash your hands, wear a clean apron, wear a hat or hair net, remove all jewellery, cover all cuts, report to the person in charge if you're ill, don't taste food with your fingers.
- Always use clean equipment.
- Avoid cross-contamination (see previous page).
- If you're defrosting frozen food before cooking it, make sure it's defrosted fully.

- Cook food at the right temperature (see below) and for long enough.
- Make sure food is cooked all the way through, e.g. cook thicker pieces of meat for longer than thin ones — test the middle to make sure it's cooked properly.

SERVING FOOD

- Serve hot food straight away.
- If you're serving food cold or storing it, cool it down as quickly as possible. Keep food covered so it's away from flies — preferably put it in the fridge.

Cook and Reheat Food to the Right Temperatures

1) Cook food thoroughly to kill bacteria — the temperature should be 72 °C or more in the middle.
2) If you're keeping food warm, keep it at about 70 °C, and don't keep things warm for more than an hour before eating.
3) If you're reheating, make sure the food is heated to at least 72 °C for at least three minutes.

Practice Questions

1) What is the main cause of food poisoning and what are the symptoms?
2) Describe the three conditions that allow bacteria to multiply very quickly.
3) A chef is preparing a Chicken Caesar Salad.
   a) Name a high-risk ingredient he is using and explain why it's high risk.
   b) Name three things the chef should do to avoid cross-contamination when preparing the salad.
   c) What temperature should the chicken in the salad be cooked to?
4) Give an example of safety and hygiene procedures you'd follow when:
   a) purchasing king prawns
   b) storing milk
   c) serving cooked rice

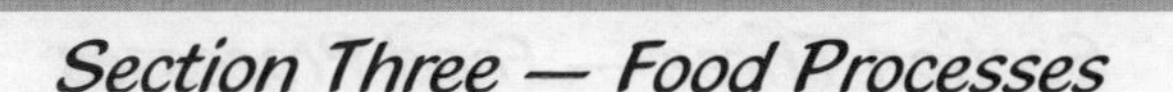

Preservation

I like to eat food straight away — but some people out there like to preserve it. Where's the fun in that...

The Right Temperature is Vital When Preserving Food

To preserve food, you need to keep it in conditions that bacteria can't grow in.
First up, there are some critical temperatures that affect bacterial growth:

Cook food ABOVE 72 °C to KILL bacteria

These preservation methods all use heat:

1) Canning — food is put into a sealed can and heated to 115 °C, killing any bacteria. Because the can is sealed, no more bacteria can get in.
2) Bottling — this is like canning but, erm, with bottles.
3) Pasteurisation — food, e.g. milk, is heated to 72 °C then carefully packaged to make sure that no bacteria contaminate the food.

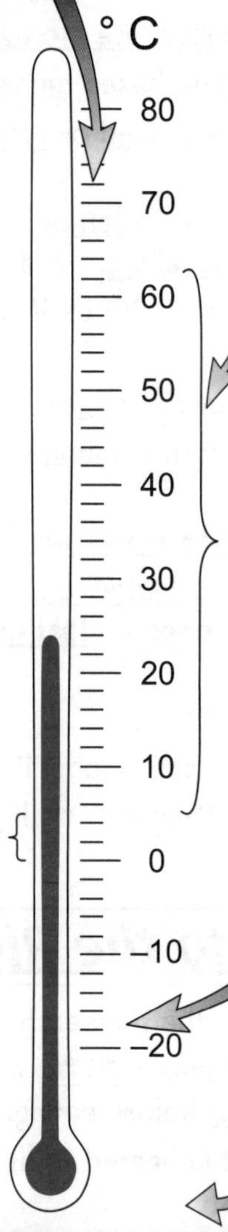

°C
80
70
60
50
40
30
20
10
0
–10
–20

The DANGER ZONE is 5 to 63 °C

1) Bacteria grow and multiply quickly in temperatures from 5 °C to 63 °C — this range of temperatures is called the danger zone.
2) The optimum temperature for bacteria growth is 37 °C.

Chill at 0 °C to 5 °C to SLOW the growth of bacteria

1) Keeping food in the fridge, between 0 °C and 5 °C, slows down the growth of bacteria.
2) This extends the shelf life of the food — although it won't last as long as canned or bottled foods do.
3) High-risk foods MUST be kept chilled to prevent the risk of food poisoning.
4) Chilling food doesn't change its properties much — chilled food looks and tastes the same — but it may have a harder texture.

Freeze food at –18 °C to STOP THE GROWTH of bacteria...

1) Freezing food at –18 °C or lower stops bacteria growing — they become dormant.
2) Freezing greatly extends the shelf life of the food and the nutrients aren't lost.
3) It doesn't kill the bacteria though. They become active again when the food defrosts.

...and to preserve COLOUR and FLAVOUR

1) Vegetables contain ripening enzymes that make them go brown when they're stored for long. To stop this you can blanch them — plunge them into boiling water to kill the ripening enzymes — and then freeze them. That way they'll keep their colour.
2) Accelerated freeze drying means quickly freezing food and then drying it in a vacuum so that the ice turns to water vapour. This method is used for instant coffee and packet soups because it keeps the colour and flavour.

Danger Zones — exam halls...

What a shame you can't preserve your revision. You could learn a page, pop the know-it-all section of your brain into the freezer and then get it out again for your exam. Oh, but better defrost it fully first...

Preservation

Don't Let Food go Past its Best

Use by date

1) The use by date is shown on products with a short shelf life, e.g. high-risk foods (see p46).
2) It's given as a safety warning. If you use the food after this date, it might not be safe — you run the risk of getting food poisoning.

Best before date

1) The best before date is shown on products with a longer shelf life, e.g. tinned foods.
2) It's given as a warning about quality. If you eat the food after this date, it's probably safe but might not be as nice as you'd expect, e.g. biscuits could be soft.

Chemicals can Preserve Food but they Alter the Taste

Bacteria can't grow if you use certain chemicals to preserve food — but this changes the taste.

- Salt — salt absorbs water from bacteria, making them shrivel up and die. Salt is used to preserve meats like ham and bacon — but it makes food taste salty. (Really, it does.)
- Sugar — using high amounts of sugar (e.g. in jam) kills bacteria in much the same way. But then of course the food tastes very sweet.

Bacteria also need a neutral pH (6.6 to 7.5) to grow — so making food acidic or alkaline can preserve it:

- Vinegar — vinegar is too acidic for bacteria to grow — but it also gives food an acidic, tangy taste and can make it look brown. Vinegar is used in chutneys and pickles.
- Concentrated lemon juice — lemon juice is also acidic. It's used to preserve fruit salads.

There are Other Methods of Preservation

1) Drying — this removes all the moisture so bacteria can't grow.
2) Irradiation — food is zapped with radiation, which kills the bacteria.
3) MAP (modified atmosphere packaging) and vacuum packaging are other methods — see page 58.

Practice Questions

1) What is meant by the danger zone?
2) What temperature do bacteria grow fastest at?
3) How can you slow the growth of bacteria? How can you stop their growth?
4) How is a use by date different from a best before date?
5) Explain why salt can be used to preserve foods.
6) Delia has made a vegetable curry. She wants to save some to give to her friends next week.
   a) Describe a way she could preserve her curry using heat.
   b) Suggest another way (not using heat) that she could preserve her curry.

Domestic and Industrial Equipment

A bad workman always blames his tools. Or is it a bad chef who always blames his whisk? Anyway, you've got loads of top tools to make use of in food technology...

Electrical Equipment has lots of Advantages

1) Electrical equipment is any piece of equipment that works using electricity (from the mains or batteries).
2) It works the same way every time — so you get consistent results.
3) You get a quality product because of accurate measurements and precise timings.
4) It's much quicker and easier to use electrical equipment (e.g. for whisking) than doing things by hand.

EXAMPLE — electronic scales are much better than traditional scales...

1) They'll weigh ingredients accurately to within 0.05 g.
2) There's less room for human error in reading a digital display than with judging when balance pans are level (or when a needle is pointing to the right number).
3) You can preset the scales to weigh different ingredients, which saves time.

Using Electrical Equipment can Improve your Product

CUTTERS

- You can use them to cut products like biscuits to exactly the same shape and size every time.

THERMOMETERS AND TEMPERATURE PROBES

- There are different types of thermometer for measuring the temperatures of rooms, ovens, fridges and freezers.
- Temperature probes are used to measure the temperature inside food, by sticking the probe right into the middle. You should use a probe with high-risk foods to check they're properly cooked (see p47).

If only we had some electrical equipment, boss.

FOOD PROCESSORS

- For slicing, chopping or dicing food.
- Using the same settings will give you the same results each time.

BLENDERS

- For blending or crushing ingredients, e.g. to make soup.
- Blenders save time and effort over doing the same task with hand tools.

BREADMAKERS/ DOUGH HOOKS

- A breadmaker (or a hook attachment for a food processor) will mix and knead bread dough.
- This saves the effort of kneading by hand — it's also more hygienic.

Eeee, there wasn't this fancy stuff around when I was young...

Manufacturers make tons and tons of consistent products, so it's no wonder they use all sorts of posh, high-tech gadgets. Learn the names of all the different pieces of equipment and the uses of each one.

Domestic and Industrial Equipment

Use the Right Equipment to Make Healthier Products

Steamers are a good way to cook food such as vegetables, instead of boiling them in water.

1) Vegetables cooked by steaming keep more of their taste, texture and colour.
2) They also keep more vitamins and minerals (lots are lost by boiling).
3) The food doesn't have to be drained so it's less likely to break up.

Microwave ovens have some advantages over traditional ovens:

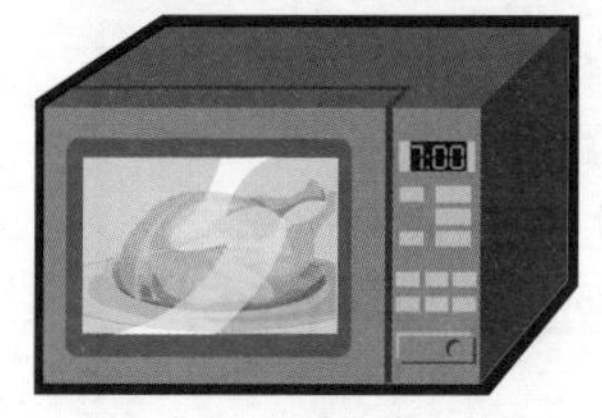

1) They can defrost, reheat and cook food quickly and evenly.
2) Food is healthier because more vitamins are retained.
3) Microwaves are more efficient — they use less energy, especially for cooking small portions.

There's Loads of Other Industrial Equipment too...

1) Industrial producers use very large ovens — e.g. biscuits are often cooked on a conveyor belt moving through a big tunnel oven.
2) Some food is cooked in vats — huge containers usually made from stainless steel.
3) A hopper is a huge holding container that can feed in the correct amount of ingredients.
4) A centrifuge works like a huge spin dryer — it separates liquids from solid parts, e.g. to make olive oil.
5) Depositors are huge tubes, nozzles or funnels which fill containers like pastry cases and moulds.

Use Equipment Safely and Hygienically

1) Always read the instructions carefully before using equipment.
2) Everyone should wash their hands both before and after using equipment.
3) All equipment needs to be thoroughly cleaned after use to prevent cross-contamination (see p46).
4) Workers should be given appropriate health and safety training — e.g. using safety guards, emergency stop buttons and regularly servicing the equipment.

Practice Questions

1) Explain why it can be better to use electrical equipment rather than make products by hand.
2) a) Name a piece of electrical equipment you could use to knead dough.
   b) What equipment would you use to measure the temperature in the middle of food?
3) Name two pieces of equipment that industrial food producers use, and say what each is for.
4) a) Imagine you're asked to bake a batch of cookies for your school fair. How would you make sure your cookies are consistent?
   b) You're also asked to bring along a potato salad. Explain how you would cook the potatoes so that plenty of nutrients are retained.

Social Issues

Manufacturers don't just make a product and hope people will buy it. They look for groups of people with specific needs or wants and then they design a product to meet consumer preferences.

You Could Aim at People with Specific Dietary Needs...

Everyone should eat a healthy, balanced diet with a little bit of everything — but some people have special requirements. Your target group (see page 5) could be people with particular dietary needs:

1) Babies and toddlers need certain nutrients for growth and development.
2) Pregnant and breastfeeding women need extra protein, calcium and iron.
3) Elderly people may need to cut down on fats and carbohydrates.
4) Athletes and people with active jobs want food that provides energy.
5) Overweight people and people with inactive jobs need to eat low-fat foods.
6) Other groups, e.g. vegetarians, diabetics and people with allergies (see p.35) also have special requirements.

EXAM TIP
You might have to explain how you'd adapt a product to make it suitable for particular groups.

...Economic Needs...

How much time and money people have influences what they buy...

1) Special offers on products attract customers who want to save money.
2) But some people only buy high-quality food, never mind how expensive it is.

...Social Needs...

1) Entertaining foods are popular with children, e.g. pasta in funny shapes, cereals with free toys.
2) Trendy foods, like sushi, can be popular. Celebrity chefs can help to boost the sales of particular products, brands or supermarkets they endorse.

3) Eating can be a social occasion — people eat out at restaurants, have family Sunday roasts or eat nibbles at a party.
4) Office workers in cities tend to nip out for a sandwich (or pasty, or whatever) at lunchtimes.
5) Convenience foods are popular with people who lead busy lives. E.g. cereal bars can be eaten on the go, ready meals can be cooked quickly, and fast food is, well, fast.

...Ethical Preferences...

See pages 54-55 for more on this.

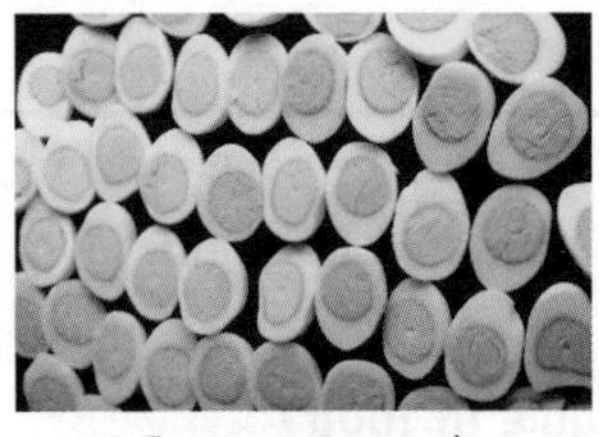
These eggs aren't freely arranged.

1) People choose to buy free-range products, like eggs and chicken, because they know the animals are treated ethically.
2) Some people prefer to buy organic foods that are grown naturally.
3) Fairtrade products, e.g. bananas, are popular with customers who want to make sure farmers get a fair price for their products.
4) Some people prefer to buy British or local produce, e.g. meat, to support the local economy and to reduce food miles (see p54).
5) Some people won't eat fish that's becoming endangered, e.g. bluefin tuna.

Runner beans — you can eat them on the go...

It's a bit freaky really. You think you're buying something of your own free will, but really there's a manufacturer somewhere going, "Ha — I knew they'd go for those low-fat, organic, owl-shaped crisps."

Social Issues

...Cultural or Religious Needs...

You should consider catering for different cultural or religious needs when picking your target group.

1) You could base a product on a traditional recipe from a target culture, e.g. an Indian samosa, a Sri Lankan fish curry, a Polish chicken soup.
2) You can cater for people who obey religious food laws by using particular ingredients. In both Islam and Judaism, for example, some foods are banned (e.g. pork) and some foods must be prepared in a particular way. Food suitable for Muslims is known as halal and food that Jews can eat is kosher. So for example you could buy meat from a halal butcher.
3) Cultural and religious festivals are a good opportunity for designers and manufacturers to make special products, e.g. mince pies at Christmas and pancakes on Shrove Tuesday.

...or just Give People What They Want

Not all target groups are to do with specific needs — personal taste can be just as important. People might like a product because:

"Go on, I'll let you try the steak first."

1) It looks good.
2) It tastes good.
3) The packaging is appealing.
4) The food is terrifically hot and spicy.
5) Some people will try anything that's new and exotic — raccoon steak, anyone...

We've got More Variety of Food Than Ever

Multicultural factors have a lot of influence on food production because they increase the variety of food:

1) You can eat food from all around the world, e.g. Chinese, Middle-Eastern, Italian food. Shops in multicultural areas tend to sell a wider variety of ingredients.
2) You get to try new flavours and spices, e.g. hot and spicy Mexican food.
3) Different cultures bring different cooking methods, e.g. stir fry, flambée (pouring brandy over something and setting fire to it — fun).

Practice Questions

1) Briefly describe the dietary needs of:
   a) babies
   b) pregnant women
   c) athletes

2) Amy is designing a range of food products targeted at rich people who work long hours.
   a) Suggest one product she could include in the range.
   b) Explain why your product would be suitable.
3) Give three examples of how ethical preferences affect what foods people buy.
4) Give two reasons why designers might want to know the religions of people in their target groups.

Environmental and Ethical Issues

Producing food, making packaging and transporting products all have a big effect on the environment. And with a growing world population, more food needs to be produced...

Food Production can Harm the Environment

RESOURCES ARE RUNNING OUT...

1) Some food resources are in short supply. For example, stocks of many popular fish are getting very low, e.g. cod, bluefin tuna.
2) Processing food uses lots of energy, which uses up resources like oil and gas.
3) Product packaging uses up resources, e.g. trees for paper, oil for plastic, metal ores for cans.

...SO WE NEED TO USE RESOURCES SUSTAINABLY

Look in the glossary for an explanation of 'sustainable.'

1) Scarce food resources, e.g. cod stocks, need to be protected.
2) Electricity produced using renewable energy, e.g. solar power, could be used for processing.
3) Less packaging could be used or packaging could be made from renewable resources. E.g. the wood pulp used to make cardboard often comes from plantations where enough trees are planted to replace those that are felled.
4) Packaging can often be reused and recycled, instead of throwing it away in landfill sites.

EXAM TIP

With questions on this kind of stuff, don't write things like "because it's bad for the environment" — explain why it's bad (or good...).

TRANSPORTING FOOD HARMS THE ENVIRONMENT...

1) Some food is transported a long way to be sold, e.g. some green beans you buy in the UK have come from Kenya. This can be expensive, and it's also bad for the environment. Planes, ships and trucks all burn scarce fossil fuels and release carbon dioxide into the atmosphere, contributing to global warming.
2) But consumers want food to be available all year round, not just when it's in season here. So shops and manufacturers buy food from abroad when it's out of season at home, e.g. asparagus has a very short season here. Also, some things just can't be grown here, like bananas.
3) Transport costs (and environmental impact) can be kept down by using packaging that stacks well — to fit as much as possible on each lorry.

A greener way to transport bananas.

...SO LOCAL AND SEASONAL FOOD IS BEST

1) To reduce food miles, some people try to only buy local products.
2) So, if you're developing a fruit tart, consider whether the fruits you intend to use are available locally and whether they're in season.

Food miles is the distance food travels from where it's produced to where it's sold.

Fair enough, but do I really have to use recycled toilet paper...

There are loads of ways to reduce the impact of food production on the environment — so make sure you know lots of examples. Learn the key terms like sustainability too (examiners love big posh words).

Environmental and Ethical Issues

Some Food Meets Environmental and Ethical Standards

Many consumers care about different environmental, ethical and social issues. So some companies develop products that meet specific standards — and they put labels on the products to show this.

Free range foods

1) Food labelled as free range lets consumers know that animals have a higher standard of welfare than in intensive farming and they're free to roam.
2) They cost more because it's a less efficient way of farming.

Fairtrade foods

1) The FAIRTRADE mark lets consumers know that farmers and workers in developing countries receive a fair price.

2) The Fairtrade Labelling Organisations International (FLO) sets Fairtrade standards and supports producers in developing countries.
3) Through Fairtrade, farmers and workers in developing countries get fair prices, decent working conditions and can invest in their communities.

Farm Assured foods

1) The Red Tractor symbol lets consumers know that the food producers meet standards of food safety, hygiene, animal welfare and environmental protection set by the Assured Food Standards scheme. (There are other similar farm assured schemes.)
2) Farm assured foods can be traced back to the farms they come from.

Organic foods

1) Food labelled as organic is grown without using any artificial pesticides or fertilisers.
2) Organic meat production has really high animal welfare standards and the animals aren't given growth hormones.
3) However, organic food production isn't as efficient — less food is produced per acre.
4) This makes it more expensive but some people are willing to pay more for food that's grown naturally.

Practice Questions

1) Give an example of a food resource that is in short supply.
2) A food processing company is concerned about environmental issues. They want to make some changes to how they make and package food.
   a) Suggest a renewable energy source that could be used to generate the electricity needed for processing food.
   b) Suggest a renewable resource they could use to make packaging.
3) What is meant by food miles?
4) Susan is buying eggs. She chooses some labelled 'free range'. What does this mean?
5) What does the Fairtrade Labelling Organisations International (FLO) do?
6) a) James buys some organic potatoes. What does organic mean?
   b) Why is organic food more expensive than food produced by intensive farming?

Labelling

Labelling on products can help people make informed choices about what they eat. Manufacturers also use labels to try to tempt customers with slogans like 'a healthy choice' and 'good value for money'.

Food Labels Can't be Misleading

Manufacturers can't just say anything they like on the label — they must obey these laws:

- Trade Descriptions Acts (1968)
- Food Labelling Regulations (1996)
- Food Safety Act (1990)
- Food Standards Act (1999)

Labels Must Tell You Certain Information by Law

The law says that the label on pre-packed food has to tell you all this stuff:

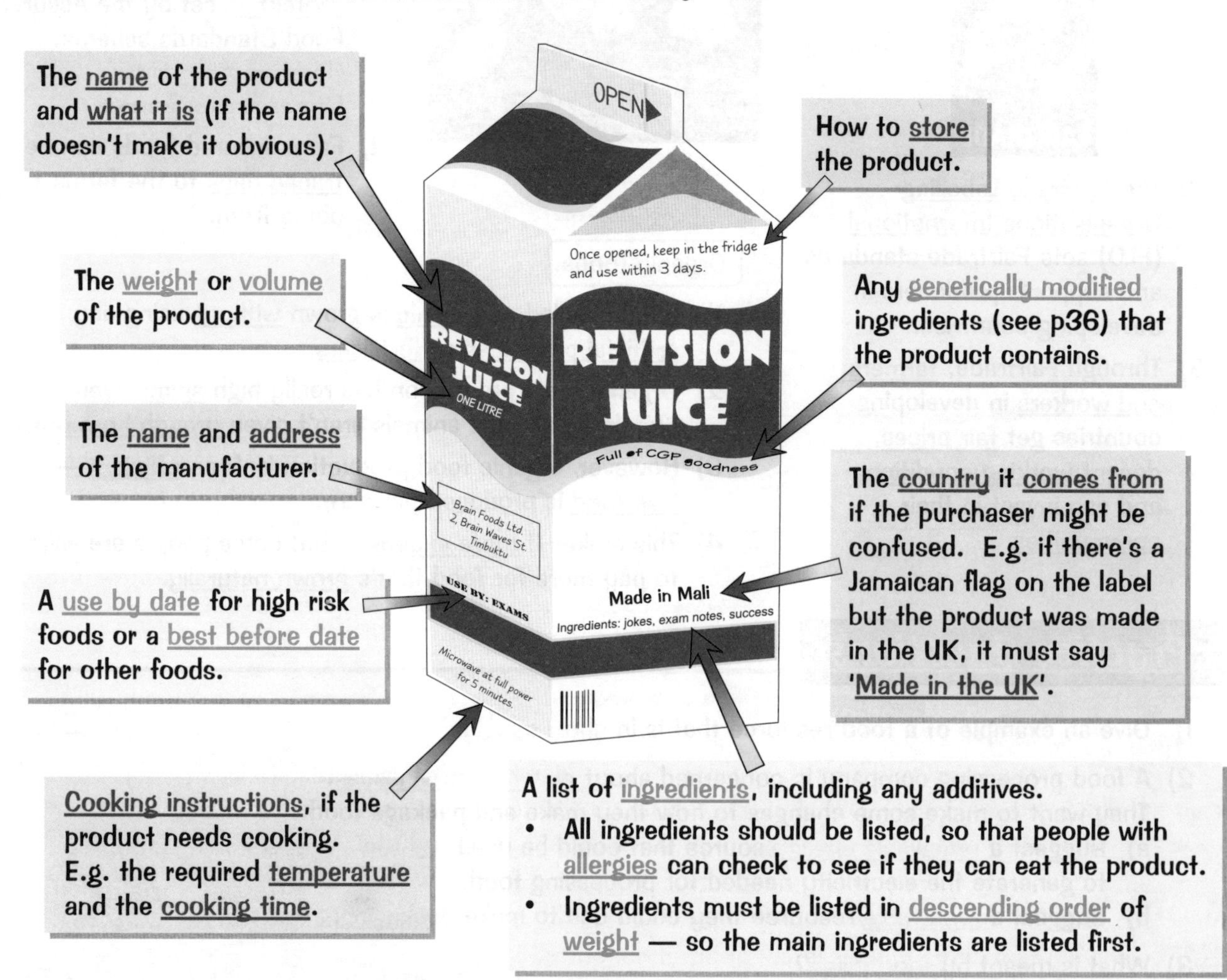

A list of ingredients, including any additives.

- All ingredients should be listed, so that people with allergies can check to see if they can eat the product.
- Ingredients must be listed in descending order of weight — so the main ingredients are listed first.

Your label can't be libel (unless you're a Brummie)...

So, only pre-packed foods need to be labelled by law. Simple. (Or is it? — a single cucumber wrapped in plastic film doesn't count as pre-packed. Hmm, I'd just say 'pre-packed' if it comes up in the exam.)

Labelling

Nutritional Information is Needed to Back up Claims

1) Lots of products list nutritional information but they don't have to by law...
2) ...UNLESS they make a special nutritional claim, such as 'low-fat' or 'high in fibre'.
3) Nutritional information is usually shown in a table listing energy content, protein, carbohydrate, etc.
4) Claims such as 'low fat' can only be made if the nutritional information backs this up.

NUTRITIONAL INFORMATION	per 100g	per 55g serving
Energy	2180kJ/525 kcal	1199kJ/289 kcal
Protein	6.5g	3.6g
Carbohydrate	50.0g	27.5g
of which sugars	2.0g	1.1g
Fat	33.0g	18.2g
of which saturates	15.0g	8.3g
Sodium	0.7g	0.4g
Fibre	4.0g	2.2g

1 kcal is 1 calorie.

There can be Other Useful Stuff on Labels too

Other information doesn't have to be there but manufacturers try to make their label useful to consumers.

Some products guarantee the food is of a high standard — or else you can claim your money back.

Symbols are used to show that food is suitable for a particular diet, e.g. food suitable for vegetarians is often shown with a green V.

The manufacturer can suggest accompaniments to the product — what kind of food it's best eaten with, e.g. a label on chutney may say it's best eaten with cold meats or cheese.

Possible allergy problems can be highlighted, e.g. 'may contain traces of nuts'.

Traffic-light labelling on a product shows how healthy it is at a glance. Red, orange and green colours show whether a product has high, medium or low amounts of saturated fat, salt and sugar. For example, a pizza might be red for saturated fat and yellow for salt and sugar.

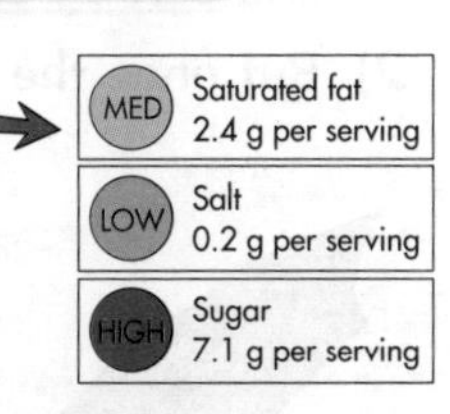

A recycling symbol means that some (or all) of the packaging can be recycled.

Some labels on take-away products warn about very hot contents.

Practice Questions

1) What kinds of food product must be labelled by law?
2) Calum is designing the label for his product. So far, he's listed the ingredients.
   a) Why is important that all of the ingredients are listed?
   b) Give five things, other than the ingredients, that the label must include.
3) a) When do manufacturers have to give nutritional information on their products?
   b) Describe how nutritional information is usually shown.
4) Many food labels include things that don't need to be there by law, e.g. 'traffic-light labelling'.
   a) What is traffic-light labelling?
   b) Give two other things that a food label might have, that don't have to be there by law.

Packaging

Packaging is pretty useful — you wouldn't want to buy your food and then have it all slopping about and mixing together in your shopping bags... Even better, some packaging can stop food going off.

Packaging Contains, Protects and Preserves Food

Most food products are packaged before they're sold:

1) To contain the product neatly.
2) To protect it from being damaged while it's being transported, displayed and stored.
3) To preserve the food and extend its shelf life — otherwise it's more likely to be wasted.
4) To avoid contamination, e.g. from flies, vermin or people touching the food.
5) To identify what the product is and to give customers useful information.

There are laws about food packaging:

1) It can't be hazardous to human health.
2) It can't cause food to deteriorate (go off).
3) It can't cause an unacceptable change in a product's quality.

Different Forms of Packaging can Extend Shelf Life

1 MODIFIED ATMOSPHERE PACKAGING (MAP)

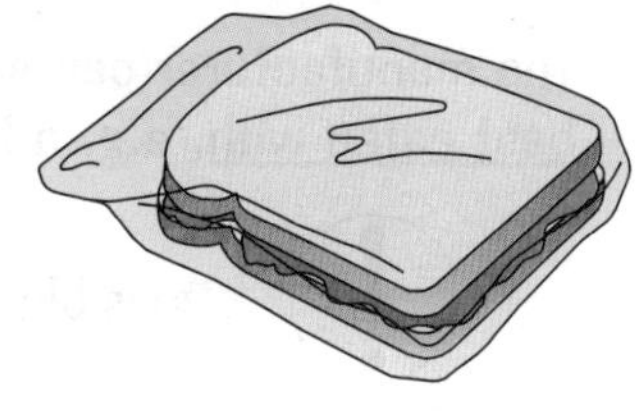

MAP extends the shelf life of fresh foods, e.g. fresh and cooked meats, fresh pasta, cheese and sandwiches.

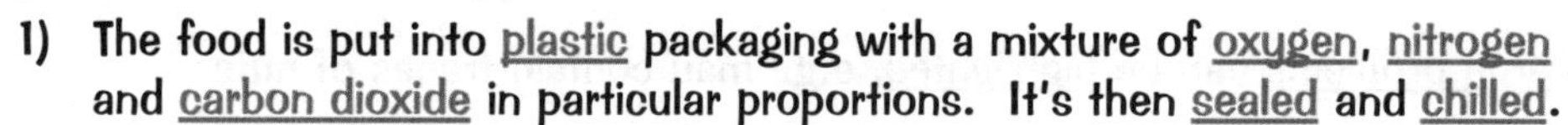

1) The food is put into plastic packaging with a mixture of oxygen, nitrogen and carbon dioxide in particular proportions. It's then sealed and chilled.

2) But once the packet's been opened, the food has a normal shelf life.

2 VACUUM PACKAGING

Vacuum packaging is often used for dry foods, e.g. coffee, and for meat and fish.

1) Food is put into plastic packaging, then the air is sucked away from around the food. It's then sealed to keep the food in oxygen-free conditions.
2) Once the packet is open you have to follow the storage instructions.

Nanotechnology can Improve Packaging Properties

Nanotechnology is a new technology that involves using very, very small particles (nanoparticles).

1) Some nanoparticles can make packaging stronger, lighter or more heat-resistant.
2) Food can be made to last longer, e.g. adding clay nanoparticles to plastic makes the packaging better at keeping out oxygen and moisture. Some nanoparticles can kill harmful microorganisms.
3) Some 'smart packaging' uses nanoparticles to change the packaging's properties depending on the conditions. E.g. a milk carton could be made to change colour when the milk goes off.

Good things come in teeny tiny nano-packaging...

Just look at all this new-fangled stuff you have to learn about. In my day, MAP was something you took with you on a long walk. But I don't suppose the examiners will be too impressed if you tell them that.

Packaging

Different Types of Material are Used for Packaging

1) Packaging uses up a lot of resources — some of which are finite (will run out eventually).
2) Manufacturing packaging uses a lot of energy.
3) However, using packaging does mean that less food is wasted — so there's a balance.
4) Using recycled material to make packaging reduces its environmental impact.

Various materials are used in different shapes and thicknesses to make packaging for different products.

GLASS, e.g. bottles, jars

- It's a strong, rigid material
- It's transparent — customers can see what they're buying
- It's resistant to high temperatures
- It can be reused and is easy and cheap to recycle

BUT...

- It's pretty heavy
- Glass breaks easily

PLASTIC, e.g. bottles, trays

- You can get rigid plastics and flexible ones
- It can be transparent or coloured
- Many types are microwavable — food can be heated in the packaging
- It's lightweight
- It can be printed on

BUT...

- Most types don't biodegrade
- Some plastic can't be recycled

CARD and PAPERBOARD, e.g. boxes, packets

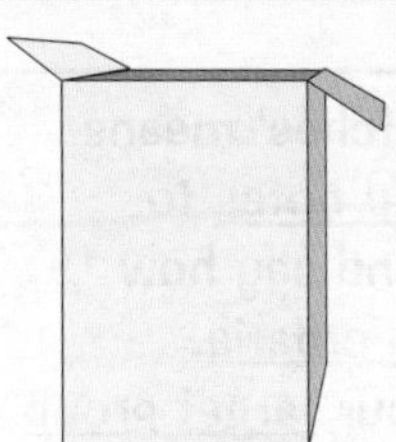

- Usually biodegradable
- Fairly strong
- Lightweight and flexible
- Easy to print on
- Waterproof if laminated
- Easy and cheap to recycle

BUT... You can't see the contents, and it's not very rigid, so the product may get squashed

METALS (aluminium, tin, steel), e.g. cans, foil

- Most metals are strong and some are fairly light e.g. aluminium.
- They're resistant to high temperatures
- Aluminium is cheaper to recycle than to extract from the ground

BUT...

- Metals can react with some foods
- You can't see the contents

Practice Questions

1) Give three reasons why packaging is used for food products.

2) Emma wants to set up a business making and selling sandwiches. She is considering what type of packaging to use.
   a) Suggest a packaging technique she could use to keep the sandwiches fresh.
   b) Outline the process used to package food this way.

3) Give two ways in which nanotechnology can be used in packaging to make food last longer.

4) Simon is deciding which material to use for his packaging.
   a) Give two advantages and two disadvantages of using glass.
   b) Give two advantages and two disadvantages of using metals.

Exam Technique

1) The exam lasts 2 hours. There's one paper split into two sections.
2) Section A is the design question. Section B is a load of questions on anything and everything you've learned — ingredients, nutrition, processes, safety, etc.

Section A is the Design Question

A bit before the exam, your teacher will give you a preparation sheet which tells you the theme of the design question. Use this to do plenty of research around the theme and practise a few designs.

Section A is about designing a new product.
You are advised to spend about 30 minutes on this question.

Design Brief

A company is developing ideas for a new snack bar.

Design Criteria

A successful product will:

- appeal to children
- be healthy
- be suitable to eat 'on the go'

1 (a) Sketch **two** design ideas for your product and annotate your sketches to show how they meet the design brief and criteria. Do not draw any packaging.

(2 x 6 marks)

The examiners suggest how long you should spend on each question — pay attention to this so you don't spend too long on a question. You should aim to spend about 1 minute per mark.

Don't draw any packaging — you won't get any marks for it.

Design 1

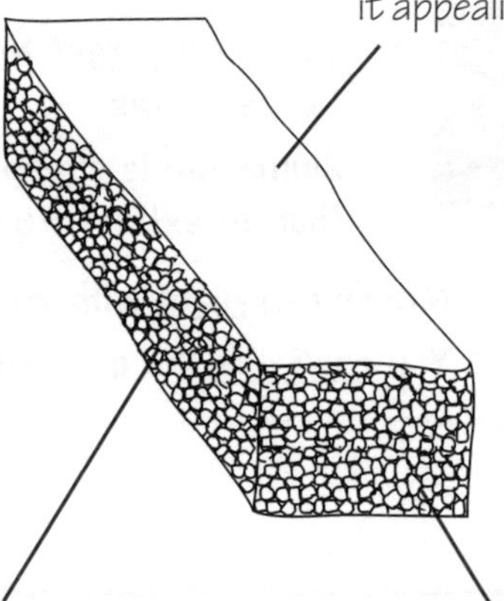

'Annotate your sketches' means that you should add notes to explain your idea and say how it meets the design criteria. E.g. think about your target group (children) and what they like.

Check you've covered all the design criteria. It helps if you tick off each one as you go.

Saying something is 'healthy' is a bit vague — give specific reasons why it's healthy.

Design 2

The cookie will have dried fruit and nut pieces...

Make sure you do the right number of sketches — read the question carefully.

Exam Technique

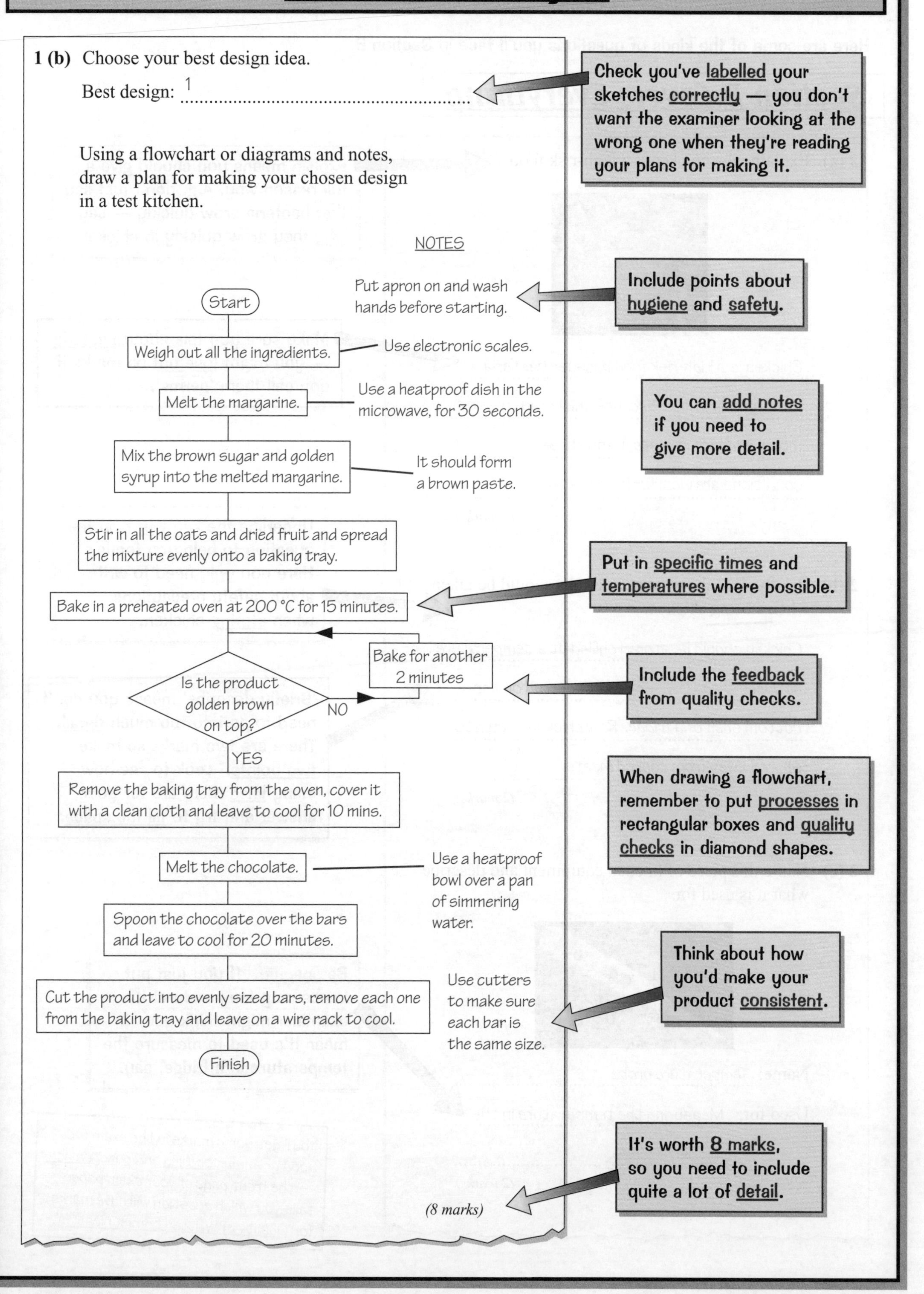

Exam Technique

Here are some of the kinds of questions you'll face in Section B.

Section B Covers Everything

2 (a) Explain why chicken is a high-risk food.

Chicken is a high-risk food because bacteria grow quickly in it — because chicken is moist and high in protein, and these conditions are ideal for bacteria to grow.

(3 marks)

Explain means you should give a full reason why, e.g. don't just say that bacteria grow quickly — say why they grow quickly in chicken.

Make sure you talk about bacteria — you might lose out on marks if you call them 'germs'.

2 (b) Briefly describe what precautions should be taken when storing chicken.

Chicken should be stored chilled at a temperature between 0 and 5 °C, sealed or covered on the bottom shelf of a fridge. Raw chicken should be stored away from cooked meats.

(2 marks)

Underline the key words in the question to help you focus. Here you only need to write about safety precautions when storing chicken.

'Briefly describe' means you don't need to go into too much detail. There are two marks so make two points. Look to see how many lines there are for your answer and try to fill the space.

2 (c) Name this piece of kitchen equipment and describe what it is used for.

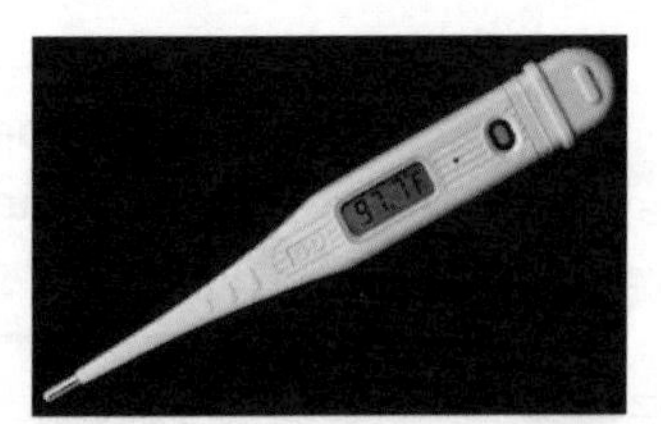

Name: *Temperature probe*

Used for: *Measuring the temperature in the middle of foods.*

(2 marks)

Be specific. If you just put 'measuring temperature' the examiner might think you mean it's used to measure the temperature in a fridge, say.

You'll get some marks in the exam for good grammar, spelling and punctuation — the front page of your exam paper tells you which question will have marks for 'Quality of Written Communication'.

Exam Technique

3 (a) A test kitchen has carried out sensory testing on two pizzas. Both pizzas had exactly the same sauce and toppings but their bases were different. The star diagrams below show the results.

Analyse the results and suggest how they might be used by manufacturers.

> **Analyse** means you need to **describe** what the data shows and **draw some conclusions**.

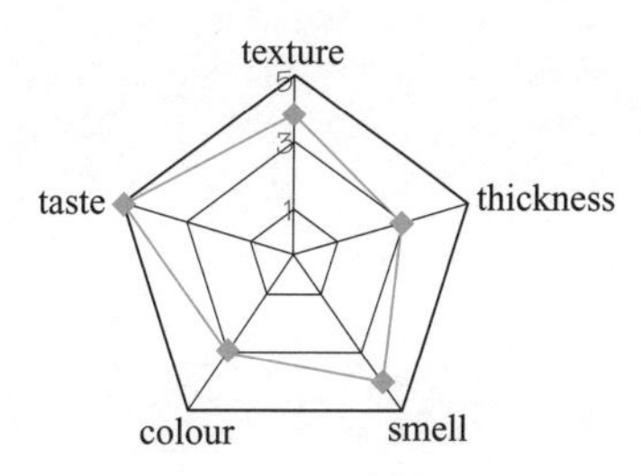

Pizza made using homemade pizza base.

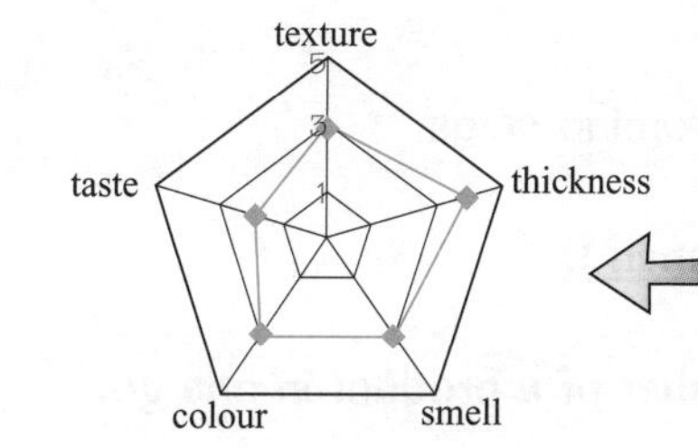

Pizza made using a standard component pizza base

> Look **carefully** at the star diagrams and make sure you **understand** what they show — don't rush straight into answering the question.

The sensory tests show that people preferred the taste, texture and smell of the homemade pizza base but they preferred the thickness of the standard component pizza base. Overall the homemade pizza scored higher marks, especially for the taste, so it's more likely to be popular with consumers. Manufacturers could use these results to develop a new pizza base which has the best qualities of both bases.

(4 marks)

> Do **everything** that the question asks — don't forget to say how the sensory tests may be used by **manufacturers** too.

3 (b) Give a reason why standard components are used in food production.

They save the manufacturer time.

(1 mark)

> The question is only worth **one mark** so you only need to put **one reason**, even if you can think of loads more. You won't get any more marks for writing loads and it just **wastes time**.

4 (a) Complete the table below to show the cause of each problem and how you would prevent it.

Problem	Cause	How to prevent this problem
Mould found on peaches	*Peaches kept for too long.*	*Buy only a few peaches at once and use them up quickly.*

(2 marks)

> Even if you think an answer is **too obvious** to be what the examiner wants, write it down anyway — some questions will be **easier** than others. There's no point looking for a complicated answer.

> *When you think you've finished the exam, go back and read over your answers to check for mistakes. You might even think of something else you could add.*

Glossary

acetic acid	The acid in vinegar.
additive	Something that's added to a food product to improve its properties.
aerate	To add air to a mixture to help make it lighter, e.g. when making cakes.
aesthetics	How a product looks.
amino acids	Proteins are made of amino acids.
ascorbic acid	Another name for vitamin C.
batch production	Making a certain number of a product in one go.
binding	Holding ingredients together so the product doesn't fall apart. For example eggs are used to bind ingredients in burgers.
biodegradable	A biodegradable material is something that rots down naturally.
CAD	Computer-aided design.
CAM	Computer-aided manufacture.
caramelisation	When sugar is heated and forms a sweet-tasting, brownish liquid.
citric acid	The acid in lemon juice.
closed question	A question with a limited number of possible answers, e.g. do you like spicy food?
coagulate	To change into a more solid state. For example if you fry an egg it coagulates.
consistent	The same every time.
contaminate	To make something dirty and unhygienic, e.g. a fly could contaminate your soup.
continuous flow	Continuous flow production means making large numbers of a product non-stop.
control point	A stage in a process where you put in a control to stop a problem occuring.
cross-contamination	Transferring bacteria from raw food to other food via work surfaces, equipment or your hands.
danger zone	The range of temperatures (5 °C to 63 °C) in which bacteria multiply very quickly.
design brief	A short statement explaining why there's a need for a new product.
design criteria	The general characteristics a product should have, e.g. "Appealing to children." A list of design criteria is sometimes called a design specification.
deteriorate	When the quality of food decreases or it 'goes off'.

Glossary

disassembly	Taking a product apart.
dormant	Inactive, a bit like a deep sleep — bacteria become dormant in frozen food.
E number	A number (e.g. E150a) given to an additive when it passes EU safety tests. The additive can then be used in food throughout the European Union.
eatwell plate	Government healthy eating guidelines in the form of a pie chart which shows how much or little of each food group your diet should contain.
emulsifier	Something that keeps an oily and watery mixture stable (stops it separating into two layers).
emulsion	A mixture of oily and watery liquids, e.g. salad dressing.
enriching	Adding something like butter or cream to a product to make it thicker and tastier.
enrobing	Coating a food product in something, e.g. a thin layer of chocolate.
enzymic browning	The reaction that happens when fruit is sliced open and left uncovered — the surfaces of the cut pieces turn brown.
Essential Amino Acids	Amino acids that the body can't make itself so you need to get them from your diet.
ethical issue	A moral issue — when many people have views about whether something's morally right or wrong.
feedback	Sending back information, often so that a person or a computer can monitor whether a process is working as it should.
fermentation	When yeast breaks down sugars to release carbon dioxide and alcohol.
finishing techniques	Techniques that are used to make the finished product look as good as possible, e.g. glazing, icing.
five a day	The Government recommends that everyone should eat at least five portions of different fruits or vegetables every day in order to be healthy.
food miles	The distance a product travels from where it's produced to where it's sold.
fossil fuels	Coal, oil and natural gas, or fuels made from them. e.g. petrol. Burning fossil fuels, e.g. for transport, releases carbon dioxide, which contributes to global warming.
functional food	A food that has been artificially modified to provide a particular health benefit on top of its normal nutritional value.
Gantt chart	A time plan that shows how long different tasks will take and the order they need to be done in.

Glossary

gel	The semi-solid structure you get when a small amount of a solid ingredient sets a lot of liquid, e.g. jelly.
gelatinisation	When starch particles swell and burst, thickening a liquid.
gelling agent	Something that causes a liquid to thicken and set as a gel.
genes	The 'instructions' for how to develop contained in all the cells of a plant or animal. Genes control the characteristics of the plant or animal, e.g. how quickly fruit ripens.
genetically modified (GM) food	Food that's had its genes altered to give it useful characteristics. For example, GM tomatoes with a longer shelf life than normal.
glazing	Adding a coating to give a product a shiny, glossy appearance.
gluten	A protein found in flour that makes dough stretchy.
Guideline Daily Amounts (GDAs)	Information about how much energy or how much of certain nutrients an average adult needs each day.
hazard	Anything that's likely to cause harm.
high-risk food	A food in which bacteria can grow quickly.
hydrogenation	A process that makes oils more solid at room temperature, e.g. to make margarine.
landfill	A landfill site is a large rubbish dump that's eventually covered over with earth.
lecithin	A natural emulsifier found in egg yolks.
manufacturer's specification	Precise instructions that tell the manufacturer exactly how to make a product.
marinate	To soak something in a mixture of things like oil, wine, vinegar and herbs, to give it more flavour.
mass production	Making large numbers of a product, often on an assembly line or conveyor belt.
model	A test version of a product that you make during the development stage.
modified starches	Starches that have been treated so that they react in a particular way in certain conditions, e.g. they're used in packet custard that thickens instantly. (Modified starches are also called smart starches.)
monosodium glutamate (MSG)	A natural flavour enhancer which boosts the existing flavour of a product and gives it a savoury taste.
nanoparticles	Very, very, very small particles of a substance. Nanoparticles of a substance often have different properties from the 'normal' substance.

Glossary

nanotechnology	A new technology that involves using nanoparticles.
non-starch polysaccharide (NSP)	Often called dietary fibre. It's a type of carbohydrate that isn't digested by your body.
nutrient	Proteins, carbohydrates, fats, vitamins and minerals are all nutrients.
nutrient deficiency	Not getting enough of a nutrient, e.g. calcium deficiency.
nutrient excess	Getting too much of a nutrient, e.g. salt excess.
one-off production	Making single products that are unique.
open question	A question that has no set answers, e.g. why don't you like puddings?
organic	Organic crops are grown without using any artificial pesticides or fertilisers. Organic meat is produced to very high welfare standards and without artificial growth hormones or the regular use of antibiotics.
palatability	How pleasant the taste of a food is.
pectin	A natural gelling agent found in some fruits.
preservative	Something added to food to slow the growth of bacteria so that food lasts longer.
preserve	To make food last longer.
product specification	A detailed description of how the product should look (including measurements) and taste — it also includes what ingredients will be used.
prototype	A full-size, one-off model of a design. A prototype is made so that you can check you're completely happy with the product before making lots of it.
quality control	Checking that the standards you've set for the quality of a product are being met.
raising agent	Something that releases bubbles of gas that expand when heated. Raising agents are used to make cake and dough mixtures rise.
Recommended Daily Amounts (RDAs)	How much of certain vitamins and minerals an average adult needs each day.
recyclable	A recyclable material is one that could be recycled fairly easily.
Red Tractor symbol	A symbol showing that food can be traced to the farm it came from and that the producers meet standards for safety, animal welfare and environmental protection.
renewable	A renewable resource is one that's replaced by natural processes as fast as it is used up by humans, e.g. softwood trees in a plantation.

Glossary

resources	Things you need to make new products, e.g. oil is a resource used to make plastic.
risk assessment	Identifying potential hazards and the precautions needed to minimise risks before work starts.
salmonella	A bacteria that causes food poisoning. It's often found in eggs and chicken.
saturated fats	A group of fats that come mainly from animal sources and are solid or semi-solid at room temperature. Eating too much of them increases your risk of heart disease.
sensory analysis	Tasting samples of food and rating how good they are in various ways, e.g. taste, texture. It's done to find out what consumers think about new or existing products.
shelf life	The length of time a product can last without going off or losing its quality.
shortening	The effect of adding fat to a floury mixture — giving a product a crumbly texture.
solution	What you get when a solid dissolves in a liquid.
standard food component	A ready-made ingredient or food part, e.g. a ready-made pizza base.
suspension	What you get when a solid is held in a liquid but doesn't dissolve.
sustainable	A sustainable process or material is one that can be used without causing permanent damage to the environment or using up finite resources, e.g. sustainable wood comes from forests where fast-growing trees are chopped down and replaced.
syneresis	When protein coagulates and squeezes the fat and water out of a food.
target group	The group of people you want to sell your product to.
tenderising	Making meat more tender so that it's easier to eat, e.g. by marinating it before cooking.
test kitchen	A kitchen used to develop new food products.
toxic	A toxic chemical is one that's harmful to health.
unsaturated fats	A group of fats that come mainly from vegetable sources and are usually liquid at room temperature.
viscous	A thick, syrupy consistency.
work order	A table or a flow chart that shows tasks in sequence.

Answers

Page 5 — Product and Market Analysis

1) Taking a product apart and examining what it's made from and how it's put together etc. (Or similar answer).
2) Any three reasonable answers, e.g. price, ingredients, nutritional information, target market, storage/cooking instructions.
3) Any five reasonable answers, e.g. poor quality ingredients; unpleasant taste, smell, texture or flavour; poor quality packaging; poor nutritional value; too expensive.
4) a) The group of people you want to sell your product to.
   b) Any reasonable answers, e.g. gender, age, job, hobbies, lifestyle, income.
   c) Any five sensible answers, e.g. you could ask about age, job, favourite fruits and/or vegetables, whether they like salad dressings, where/when they eat salads.
5) Any three sensible suggestions, e.g. favourite ingredients, what kind of bread people like to eat with soup, whether they like thick or watery soup.

Page 7 — Market Research

1) Any sensible answers, e.g.
   c) Do you like cheese in your sandwiches?
   b) What kind of fillings do you like?
   c) Which of the following types of bread do you like? White; brown; wholemeal; rye.
2) Advantage: interviews can give you more detailed information than questionnaires. Disadvantage: it's harder to analyse the information from interviews. (Other answers are possible.)
3) To rate which foods taste/smell/look best. / To find out what consumers think about new or existing products.
4) (1) Ranking or rating testing, where people are asked to rank a number of similar products. (2) Star diagrams, where people rank characteristics of a product on a scale of 1-5. (3) Triangle testing, where testers try to work out which one of three products is new or different from the others. (Or similar descriptions.)
5) a) The colour and texture (and possibly size).
   b) The smell and the taste.

Page 9 — Design Criteria

1) Because they need to make sure they're making a product that people really want.
2) It explains why there's a need for a new product — it gives information about the context, who it involves, why the product is needed and how it will be used. The design brief is important because it's the starting point for the development of the product.
3) The most popular type of pasta is spaghetti, followed by ravioli. Penne and tagliatelle are less popular. People are more concerned with how the pasta dish tastes than how healthy it is. (Or similar answer.)
4) A list of requirements that say what the product should be like.
5) E.g. the dessert should:
   - be sweet and chocolate flavoured
   - be low in calories
   - have a fairly solid texture

Page 11 — Generating Proposals

1) Work from an existing product, use brainstorming. (Other answers are possible.)
2) Compare them with the design criteria, decide which ones are good and sketch and annotate them.
3) Any three sketched and annotated ideas that match the criteria given in the question.
4) By checking which one most closely matches the design criteria.
5) Nutritional analysis software.

Page 13 — Product Specification

1) Answer depends on the sketched idea chosen but should include detailed and specific information about the product.
2) To give you exclusive rights to develop your product.
3) Yes, but they need your permission and they have to pay you for it.
4) Any three reasonable answers, e.g. shape, colour, texture, new ingredient, recipe, production process, product packaging. (Other answers are possible.)

Page 15 — Development

1) Making different versions of a product to test and evaluate.
2) a) Any three sensible suggestions, e.g. use taste-testing to check the flavour, use triangle testing to see if it tastes as good as higher-fat products, use star diagram testing to check the texture, appearance, smell etc.
   b) Any two reasonable answers, e.g. change the proportions of ingredients, change the cooking method.
3) B is correct.
4) Any three sensible suggestions, e.g. try a different kind of dough for the pizza base, use fresher toppings, add olive oil.
5) a) The product specification.
   b) The design specification/design criteria.

Page 17 — Manufacturer's Specification

1) The working drawing should look something like the following:

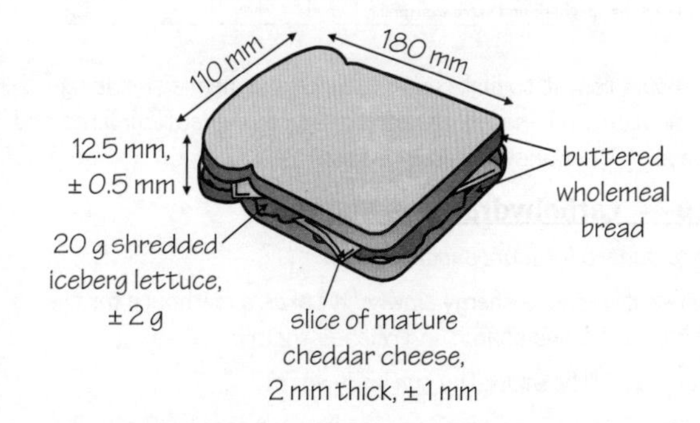

Ingredients list: cheese, lettuce, bread, margarine/butter.

2) It means that each cake could weigh up to 3 g less or 3 g more than 52 g. / It means that each cake must weigh between 49 g and 55 g.
3) a) It helps to plan each task in sequence.
   b) It helps to plan the timing of tasks.

Answers

4) Answers should look something like the following:

a)

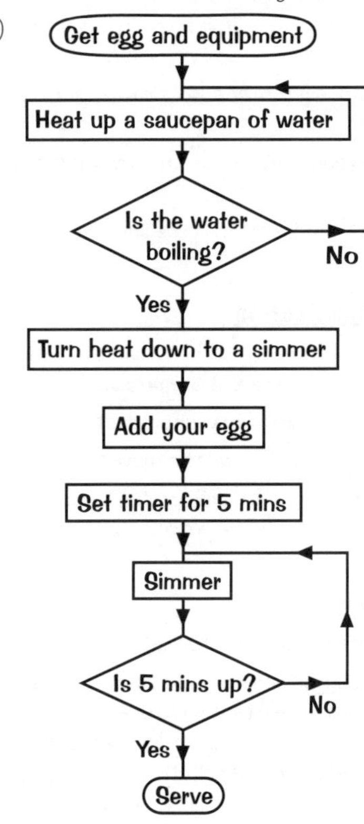

b)

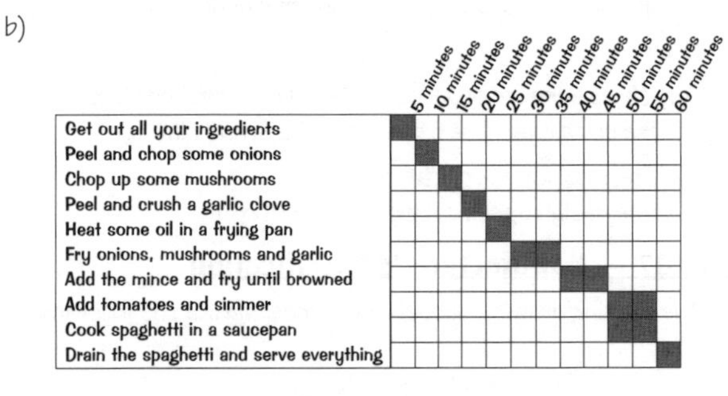

5) You should test it to make sure it works and meets the design specification. You may also want to use more questionnaires and surveys. (Other answers are possible.)

Page 19 — Carbohydrates — Sugar

1) Simple sugars (or monosaccharides).
2) Because it releases energy slowly / it takes a few hours for the body to digest the starch and release energy.
3) The energy will be stored by the body as fat.
4) E.g. granulated sugar, caster sugar, brown sugar, icing sugar.
5) a) It acts as a preservative.
   b) It speeds up fermentation.
   c) It adds sweetness and colour.
6) Any two of, e.g. they're better for your teeth / they contain fewer calories / they might be diabetic.

Page 21 — Carbohydrates — Starch

1) a) The starch granules swell.
   b) It provides bulk. / It can cause gelatinisation/thickening on heating.
2) a) It is when heat and moisture are added to starch particles, breaking the particles open and making the mixture thick and viscous.
   b) 80 °C — 100 °C
3) The starch is mixed with liquid to form a suspension. The mixture is stirred and heated, causing gelatinisation, which makes the mixture thicker.
4) a) Syneresis is when protein coagulates, squeezing out the fat and water. It can be prevented by using modified starches which allow reheating without syneresis, keeping the moisture in.
   b) 1. Pre-gelatinised starch is useful because it thickens instantly when mixed with hot water, e.g. instant noodles.
   2. Some modified starches are unaffected by acid, so they can be used to thicken acidic products, e.g. salad cream.
5) Gluten.

Page 23 — Proteins — Meat, Poultry and Fish

1) For growth and repair of muscles, tissues and organs, and to help children grow.
2) Three of, e.g. meat / fish / eggs / milk / soya beans.
3) a) Two of, e.g. B vitamins / iron / zinc.
   b) E.g. thiamin (vitamin B1) and niacin (vitamin B3).
4) To tenderise the meat (by partly breaking down the fibres).
5) Advantage: e.g. they provide lots of protein / they contain lots of B vitamins / they are fairly low in saturated fat.
   Disadvantage: e.g. they can cause salmonella.
6) Oily fish, e.g. mackerel. White fish, e.g. cod. Shellfish, e.g. prawns. (Other examples are possible.)
7) Answers may vary but should include reference to the fact that the protein vegetarians don't get from eating meat must be replaced by eating beans/nuts/lentils or alternative protein foods such as tofu, TVP, Quorn™ and others.
8) a) Soaking something in a mixture of things like oil and herbs before cooking it, to flavour it.
   b) Because alternative protein foods often don't have much flavour of their own.

Page 25 — Proteins — Eggs

1) E.g. protein, fat, vitamins A, B2 and D, iodine.
2) a) The protein in egg white stretches when it's beaten, trapping air, e.g. in cakes.
   b) Coagulation makes the ingredients stick together, e.g. in burgers.
   c) The egg white coagulates, helping foods set and stay 'thickened', e.g. in quiche.
3) a) The yolk.
   b) Mayonnaise is an emulsion. Egg yolk is used to stop the oily and watery parts of the emulsion separating.
4) E.g. 1. Always cook eggs thoroughly. 2. Make sure chicken is cooked properly. 3. Use dried or pasteurised eggs.
5) Because fried eggs absorb a lot of fat from the oil they're cooked in.
6) Many silly answers possible.

Page 27 — Fats and Oils

1) 1. Butter, made from churning cream.
   2. Margarine, made from blending vegetable oils with other ingredients.
   3. Lard, made from pig fat.
   4. Suet, made from fat around animals' organs.
   5. Oils, made from pressed seeds.
   6. Low-fat spreads, from vegetable oils and water.

Answers

2) a) 1. Butter can be used to add flavour. 2. Fat mixed with flour helps to shorten pastry, i.e. make it crumbly. 3. Butter can add colour to pastry.
   b) 1. For deep frying of, e.g. chips. 2. Enriching a sauce, i.e. adding flavour and thickness. 3. Making an emulsion, e.g. in vinaigrette. (Other answers possible.)
3) E.g. A diet with no fat would be unhealthy as the person would get less vitamins and fatty acids, which are needed to keep the body healthy.
4) a) Saturated fats come mainly from animals sources, whereas unsaturated fats are mainly from vegetable sources. Also, saturated fats are solid or semi-solid at room temperature, whereas unsaturated fats are liquid.
   b) Saturated fats: any two from, e.g. meat / butter / suet / dripping / lard.
   Unsaturated fats: any two from, e.g. sunflower oil / olive oil / rapeseed oil / peanut oil / corn oil / soya oil.
   c) Saturated fat.
   d) E.g. it can increase the risk of heart disease.
5) Cholesterol, cholesterol, cholesterol, cholesterol, cholesterol, cholesterol, cholesterol, cholesterol, cholesterol, cholesterol, cholesterol, cholesterol, cholesterol, cholesterol, cholesterol, cholesterol, cholesterol [bang].

Page 29 — Vitamins and Minerals

1) Liver, fish, butter, fish oils, eggs and yellow/orange fruit and vegetables. We need it for good eyesight and healthy tissues.
2) 1. B(1), thiamin, is useful because it helps the nervous system and the release of energy from carbohydrates.
   2. B(2), riboflavin, is useful because it helps with the release of energy and repair of tissues.
   3. B(3), niacin, is useful because it helps with the release of energy.
   4. Folic acid is useful because it's needed for growth. (Other answers are possible.)
3) Vitamin C. It protects the body from infections and allergies, helps to absorb minerals and keeps blood vessels healthy.
4) From oily fish and eggs in the diet and from exposure to sunlight. A lack of it can lead to bone diseases, e.g. rickets.
5) a) Any five from, e.g. milk, tofu, salmon, green leafy vegetables, hard water, white bread.
   b) We need it to make our bones and teeth strong, and to keep muscles and nerves healthy.
6) It helps to form haemoglobin, which is needed for healthy blood. It's found in, e.g. spinach and liver.
7) Any six from, e.g. vitamin C / vitamin A / vitamin B / dietary fibre / iron / calcium / protein.
8) 1. a) When fruit and veg is peeled.
      b) Peel as late as possible before cooking and eating, or don't peel at all.
   2. a) Chopping fruit and veg into small pieces.
      b) Chop into large pieces or use whole .
   3. a) If fruit and veg are in water, nutrients dissolve into the water.
      b) Don't leave them to stand in water.
9) Sam should eat more foods that contain calcium, e.g. milk - this will make his bones stronger. He should also eat more fruit and veg, as these contain vitamin C that will help his body fight infections. (Other answers are possible but they should focus on naming foods that will help with the particular problems mentioned in the question.)

Page 31 — Additives

1) Something that's added to a food product to improve its properties.
2) The additive can be used throughout the European Union because it's passed a safety test.
3) a) To make the food last longer.
   b) To make food look more attractive / to add colour to something colourless /to return colour that's been lost during processing.
   c) To thicken products, so they set as a gel.
   d) To keep food products stable / to stop oily and watery liquids separating.
4) a) MSG (monosodium glutamate).
   b) A sweetening agent, e.g. sugar or saccharin.
5) a) Yeast.
   b) Baking powder, bicarbonate of soda.

Page 33 —Acids and Alkalis

1) E.g. texture and appearance (other answers are possible).
2) A sharp, sour flavour.
3) Bitter and unpleasant.
4) a) Vinegar.
   b) Cornflour.
5) a) Lemon juice.
   b) Lemon juice stops enzymic browning, which turns fruits brown when they're sliced. Dipping slices of fruit into lemon juice will help make the fruit salad look fresh.
6) a) Raising agent / to make mixtures rise.
   b) Gingerbread, chocolate cake (or other cakes/biscuits with a strong flavour).

Page 35 — Healthy Eating

1) 1. Fruit and vegetables. 2. Starchy foods. 3. Dairy foods. 4. Non-dairy proteins. 5. Fatty/sugary foods.
2) You could look at the product label to check what percentage of the guideline daily amount (GDA) of fat the product provides.
3) Peter meets the eatwell plate guidelines by eating lots of starchy foods, e.g. the wholemeal toast, sandwich bread and rice. He eats some dairy foods, e.g. cheese in his sandwich and his yogurt. He eats some non-dairy sources of protein, e.g. egg in his sandwich and chicken in the curry. But he eats no fruit or vegetables, which he should eat a lot of. He eats far too much sugary and fatty food like jam, a chocolate bar, crisps, chocolate and cake.
4) a) Without enough protein the body can't grow and repair itself, which could cause restricted growth in children or muscle wastage.
   b) Eating too much sugar can lead to obesity, Type 2 diabetes and can cause tooth decay.
5) a) She could replace the beef with another source of protein, e.g., lentils or Quorn™.
   Or she could make a vegetable lasagne instead.
   b) Her friend can't tolerate eating gluten, which is found in wheat so she can't eat normal pasta. Susie could use gluten-free pasta sheets in her lasagne.

Page 37 — New Technology

1) A food that has been artificially changed to have useful characteristics by having its genes altered.

Answers

2) The crops won't get eaten by pests so more will be harvested / they'll produce a bigger yield.
3) a) Any three from, e.g. crops can be made to grow quickly / producers can get a higher yield of crops for the same amount of seed and fertiliser / more efficient production makes foods cheaper to producers and consumers / long-life foods can be grown so food has a longer shelf life and less food is wasted / foods can be made to ripen earlier than normal so fresh foods can be available for consumers earlier in the year.
   b) Any two from: GM foods haven't been around for long so their long-term health effects aren't known / there are concerns that modified genes could get out into the wider environment and cause problems / GM producers can't sell their food everywhere because the European Union restricts the import of some GM foods.
4) All foods that are GM or contain more than 1% GM ingredients must be clearly labelled.
5) a) An everyday food that has been artificially modified to provide a particular health benefit, on top of its normal nutritional value.
   b) Any two from: They can have nutrients added to them (e.g. fruit juices with calcium). / The producer can be fed a nutrient-rich diet (e.g. hens producing eggs high in omega-3). / They can have their genes altered (e.g. Golden Rice is genetically modified to contain carotene, which provides vitamin A).
6) a) The ingredients and nutritional information.
   b) Calcium.

Page 39 — Combining Ingredients

1) An oily and watery liquid mixed together (so that droplets of one are dispersed in the other).
2) a) egg yolk (lecithin)
   b) jelly / mousse / cheesecake / jam
3) A solution is a solid dissolved in a liquid.
   A suspension is a solid held (not dissolved) in a liquid.
4) a) 1. She could use less butter/margarine in the pastry.
   2. She could use less pastry to make the apple pie.
   b) The texture/taste/colour of the pastry might not be so good. If she uses less pastry the base might not be thick enough to support the pie filling.

Page 41 — Standard Food Components

1) a) E.g. ready-to-roll icing / marzipan
   b) Any two from, e.g. pizza base / tomato puree / processed meat / grated cheese
2) a) Because the raw chicken is stored and prepared somewhere else.
   b) Ready-made frozen or chilled pastry — it saves time / the manufacturer doesn't need to prepare it themselves / to make the product consistent / the staff won't need training in how to make pastry.
   c) Any sensible advantage not already given in b).
3) Any two from: the manufacturer can't pick and choose exactly what they want / it's not always reliable / the product may not be as tasty as one made with fresh ingredients / there's extra packaging and transport involved so it might be bad for the environment / extra space might be needed to store the components.
4) Any three from: sausage / bread bun / tomato ketchup / mustard.

Page 43 — Scale of Production

1) Large numbers/quantities of a product are made using a production line.
2) Computer-aided manufacture.
3) They can use CAD to produce 2D and 3D images of the product and its packaging. Once the product's been drawn on screen the design can easily be changed and values recalculated, and it's much quicker and more accurate than re-drawing designs on paper.
4) a) Batch production — because lots of sandwiches can be made in one go so it's quick, and you can change between making batches of different kinds of sandwiches.
   b) One-off production / jobbing production.
5) a) Non-stop production / production 24 hours a day.
   b) It keeps production costs per product really low for products that are sold in large numbers.
   c) It's very expensive to set up because very specialised equipment is needed / if anything goes wrong, it takes time to get it going again and unproductive time costs money.
   d) Any two from, e.g. production costs are lower / production is quicker / staff don't need to handle food as much so it's more hygienic / the product will be more consistent.

Page 45 — Quality Control

1) A product that is the same every time.
2) Setting standards and making sure they're met.
3) So the problem can be fixed quickly / ingredients aren't wasted / time and money aren't wasted.
4) Production stops while the problem is investigated and solved. E.g. the weighing scales may be slightly out so the flapjacks are ending up slightly smaller. The weighing scales would be re-set and production restarted.
5) a) Make quality control checks at all stages of food production and at the end / use visual checks / use tasting checks / by using feedback to correct any problems.
   b) The chicken could be contaminated with bacteria/salmonella.
   c) Use bought-in standard component chicken / monitor the temperature at which the chicken is stored to make sure it's between 0 °C and 5 °C / check that the chicken is cooked thoroughly / test random samples of the product after cooking to make sure it's not contaminated with salmonella.

Page 47 — Food Contamination and Bacteria

1) Eating food that's contaminated by bacteria.
   Symptoms include sickness, diarrhoea, stomach cramps, fever.
2) Moisture, warmth, neutral pH.
3) a) Chicken/sauce/eggs. They're high-risk foods because they're moist and high in protein, so bacteria grow quickly in them.
   b) Any three from: keep the knives and the chopping boards separate from anything else he's preparing / wash his hands thoroughly after handling raw meat/eggs/sauce / never store raw meat and cooked meat together / don't let the blood and juices of raw meat drip onto other food.
   c) 72 °C or more in the middle of the chicken.
4) a) Buy them from a reputable supplier / use them before their use by date / check the packaging hasn't been damaged.
   b) Follow the storage instructions/keep it in the fridge / use old purchases before they go out of date / keep cartons sealed.
   c) Serve hot rice straight away / if serving rice cold then cool it down as quickly as possible and keep it covered.

Answers

Page 49 — Preservation

1) The range of temperatures that bacteria grow and multiply very quickly in — between 5 and 63 °C.
2) 37 °C
3) Growth is slowed by chilling food below 5 °C.
Growth is stopped by freezing food at –18 °C or below, or using any method that kills the bacteria, e.g. high temperatures.
4) If you use food after the use-by date it might not be safe/might give you food poisoning. If you use food after the best-before date, it should be safe but might not be as nice as you'd expect.
5) Salt absorbs water from the bacteria, which kills them.
6) a) canning/bottling
b) Drying / irradiation / modified atmosphere packaging (MAP)/ vacuum packing / freezing.

Page 51 — Domestic and Industrial Equipment

1) Because electrical equipment works the same way every time so you get consistent results. You also get a quality product because of accurate measurements and precise timings, and it's much quicker and easier.
2) a) A bread maker / a food processor with a dough hook.
b) A temperature probe.
3) Any two from, e.g. tunnel ovens — for cooking on a conveyor belt / vats — for cooking large quantities / hopper — for holding ingredients and feeding in the correct amount / centrifuge — for separating solids from liquids / depositors — for filling pastry cases, etc.
4) a) Use cutters to make all cookies the same shape and size. / Use a thermometer to measure the temperature of the oven and bake all cookies at the same temperature. / Use a timer to make sure that all cookies are baked for the same length of time.
b) Steam or microwave the potatoes to keep more vitamins and minerals than boiling them.

Page 53— Social Issues

1) a) Babies need certain nutrients for growth and development.
b) Pregnant women need extra protein, calcium and iron.
c) Athletes need foods that provide lots of energy.
2) a) Any type of luxury product that's ready to eat or quick to cook, e.g. smoked pheasant salad.
b) The high quality/luxurious nature of the product may appeal to rich people. The speed of preparation should appeal to busy people.
3) Any three from, e.g. some people buy free range foods because they know that the animals have been treated ethically. / Some people buy organic foods because they prefer food that's been produced naturally/meat that's been produced to high welfare standards. / Some people buy Fairtrade products because they want farmers to get a fair price. / Some people buy British/local produce to support the local or national economy/reduce food miles. / Some people don't buy foods from animals that are becoming endangered, e.g. bluefin tuna.
4) Some religious groups don't eat certain foods, e.g. Muslims don't eat pork. Some religions require certain foods to be prepared in a particular way.

Page 55 — Environmental and Ethical Issues

1) e.g. cod / bluefin tuna
2) a) E.g. solar power / wind power / hydroelectricity / tidal power
b) E.g. wood pulp from a plantation where trees are replaced could be used to make paper/cardboard.
3) The distance a food travels from where it's produced to where it's sold.
4) The hens have a higher standard of welfare than they do in intensive farming and are free to roam.
5) It supports disadvantaged workers in developing countries and helps to improve working conditions and increase the sustainability of farming practices.
6) a) Food is grown without using artificial pesticides or fertilisers.
b) Organic food production isn't as efficient — less food is produced per acre.

Page 57 — Labelling

1) pre-packed foods
2) a) So that people with allergies can check to see if they can eat the product.
b) Any five from, e.g. the name of the product / the weight/ volume / the name and address of the manufacturer / cooking instructions / storage instructions / a use by date/best before date / the country it comes from.
3) a) It's needed on products that make a nutritional claim, e.g. 'low-fat'.
b) In a table listing energy content, protein, carbohydrate, etc., with values per 100 g and per serving.
4) a) Red, orange and green colours show whether a product has high, medium or low amounts of saturated fat, salt or sugar.
b) Any two of, e.g. symbols to show the food is suitable for a specific diet / allergy advice / suggested accompaniments / recycling symbols / guarantees that the food is of a high standard / warning about hot contents.

Page 59 — Packaging

1) Any three of, e.g. to contain the product neatly / to protect the product from damage when it's transported/displayed / to preserve the food / to avoid contamination / to identify what the product is / to give customers useful information
2) a) modified atmosphere packaging (MAP)
b) The food is put into plastic packaging with a mixture of oxygen, nitrogen and carbon dioxide in specific proportions. It's then sealed and chilled.
3) E.g. Adding clay nanoparticles makes the packaging better at keeping out oxygen and moisture. Some nanoparticles can kill harmful microorganisms.
4) a) Advantages — it's strong and rigid / it's transparent so customers can see the product / it's resistant to high temperatures / it can be reused and recycled.
Disadvantages — it's pretty heavy / it breaks easily.
b) Advantages — they're strong / they're resistant to high temperatures / they're cheaper to recycle than to extract.
Disadvantages — metals can react with some foods / customers can't see the contents.

Index

Index

Index